A Fellwalker's Notes

Walking the English Lake District

John Swanson

Published by Green Path Publishing

Edited by Georgia Laval

Copyright © 2016 John Swanson

ISBN: 978-0-9935369-0-8

AN EXPLANATION

As the text for this book was being finalised, late in 2015, the Lake District was overwhelmed by catastrophic flooding – the third time this has happened in eleven years and the worst occurrence yet. This made me hesitate, because it seemed in poor taste, to say the least, to produce a book that is really all about how much I've enjoyed the Lakes at a time when the people living there were suffering so much.

However, in the longer term, one thing that would make their predicament much worse would be if visitors stayed away. Much of the area's economy depends on tourism: the walkers, climbers, dawdlers and viewers. One way or another they all put money into the local economy, keeping businesses running and supporting employment. So, my modest hope is that this book might contribute in a small way by showing readers how wonderful the place is and encouraging them to go to see for themselves – not at some distant date in the future but as soon as possible.

CONTENTS

ACKNOWLEDGEMENTS

The author is grateful to Frances Lincoln for permission to quote from Wainwright's Guides to the Lakes on pages 169 and 177. Both quotes are from *A Pictorial Guide to the Lakeland Fells: Book Four, The Southern Fells* by Alfred Wainwright, published by Frances Lincoln Ltd, copyright © 2003 The Wainwright Estate. Reproduced by permission of Frances Lincoln Ltd.

The Lake District

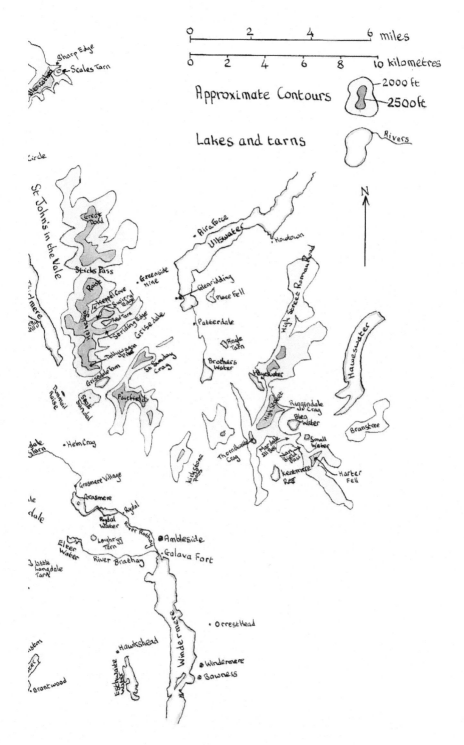

Approximate Contours
2000 ft
2500 ft

Lakes and tarns

Rivers

N

St John's in the Vale

Sharp Edge
Scales Tarn
Blencathra

circle

Great Dodd

Sticks Pass

Aira Force
Ullswater
Howtown

High Street Roman Road

Greenside Mine
Raise
Keppel Cove
Swirral Edge
Helvellyn
Red Tarn
Striding Edge
Grisedale
Dollywagon Pike
Grisedale Tarn
St Sunday Crag

Glenridding
Place Fell

Patterdale

Angle Tarn

Brothers Water

Hawes Water

Nethermost Pike
Seat Sandal
Dollywaggon
Fairfield

Haweswater

Riggindale Crag
Blea Water
High Street

Branstree

dale Tarn

Helm Crag
Grasmere Village
Rydal
Rydal Water
River Rothay
Loughrigg Tarn
River Brathay
Elter Water

Kirkstone Pass
Thornthwaite Crag

Mardale Ill Bell
Nan Bield Pass
Small Water
Kentmere Reservoir
Harter Fell

le dale

Grasmere
Ambleside
Galava Fort

Little Langdale Tarn

Windermere

Orrest Head

Hawkshead
Esthwaite Water
Windermere
Bowness

Brantwood

iii

1   INTRODUCTION

I was born in the North East of England in the 1950s. When I was about five years old my family moved to St Bees on the coast of what was then called Cumberland. Later we moved to Cockermouth, a town with two rivers, a brewery, Wordsworth's birthplace, and views of the Lake District mountains in the near distance.

Although we only lived there for about four years, to a child it seemed much longer, and I loved it. In St Bees there were fields and farms, a huge expanse of beach and sandstone cliffs with tumbled rocks to play on. In Cockermouth there were barns to explore, more fields to run in, a talking magpie, and a waterfall where our kindly schoolteacher took us to watch the salmon struggling upstream to their spawning grounds.

And in both places there were the mountains, looming blue and hazy on the horizon. My parents were not great walkers, but they had a car[1], and they would use it to visit the classic beauty spots: Grange, Buttermere and the Wastwater screes. But there was no fellwalking. That came later when I was seventeen, long after the family had returned to the North East, and I went back to the Lakes with a group of friends for two weeks' Youth Hostelling. There were five of us, and we took the coach from Newcastle to Keswick. As we snaked down the west side of the Pennines from Alston, the glorious mountains appeared, shimmering and glinting in the sunshine far away across the Eden Valley. It was a sight that had, in a way, an effect on me much as the view from Orrest Head had on Wainwright many years before.

Later came university, followed by work in London. This was when I started going back to the Lakes with a group of university friends. We would hire a house for a week, usually in the spring, and go on long walks each day, all except one when we would visit oddities like the Sellafield visitors' centre, or the Laurel and Hardy museum in Ulverston.

It was during these visits that I learned to appreciate Wainwright's books. It was one of my fellow walkers who brought them along, and at first I disliked them. I found the drawings confusing, and it seemed clumsy to carry a hardback book around all day when a good Ordnance Survey map and compass was all you needed. But in time I came to understand their appeal: the detailed pen work; the hand-written text that even then seemed dated in style but which could be very funny; and most of all the sheer authority of the books, built on many years of experience.

This set up a lifelong love of the Lakes and a habit of returning year after year. In time I started to reflect on how my relationship with the place was all one-way: I'd go there, walk, have fun, and leave. Slowly the idea of doing something more creative formed, and after many false starts, this book is the result.

It is certainly a book about walking in the Lake District, but it isn't a guidebook in the usual sense. I have written about some walks in detail, some less so; all of them have been re-walked in the past two or three years to refresh memory and provide detail, and while I have tried to include at least one walk in each of the main geographic areas, I have not attempted anything like a complete catalogue. This is not Wainwright V2.0. I have also written about and drawn other things that caught my interest and which I hope will interest readers and visitors too. There are, as I quickly learned, only so many ways of writing about climbing a fell.

Some of the drawings were done on the spot, but this is not always

---

[1] That might not seem exceptional today, but I can remember children at school bragging because they had *been in a car*.

practical; the wind rips away the paper, the rain makes it too wet to draw on or it's too cold. So, many of them were drawn back at home using a mix of sketches done quickly in situ, photographs, and a degree of imaginative license.

The maps are all hand-drawn, are approximate, and intended to show where the things I've written about can be found. As should be obvious, they are not to be used for walking: for that, the OS maps are still unbeatable.

2 GREAT LANGDALE

If Great Langdale had a lake it would be perfect; as it is, it's sublime, a classic glacial valley, cutting a long and graceful curve from the old mining village of Chapel Stile in the east to the isolated Stool End Farm in the west, where it divides into two, with Oxendale leading off to the south-west, Mickleden to the north-west, and The Band mediating between them.

The valley is surprisingly broad, with a striking contrast between the steep, rugged sides of the surrounding fells and the wide billiard-table flatness of the valley's bottom, a consequence of its glacial origins and the labour of many generations of farmers in their constant struggle to hold back the disruptive efforts of nature. The valley bottom is criss-crossed with stone walls enclosing rich grassland, but just beyond those walls the vegetation changes abruptly; out there, a more unruly gardener is in charge.

The north side of the valley is dominated by the Langdale Pikes, one of the most distinctive and well-known sights in the Lakes, easily recognised from many distant viewpoints.

One of the classic views of the Langdale Pikes, seen from Elterwater. This was drawn on the spot, one freezing cold day. Elterwater lake and village are both very pretty, but the village is almost entirely given over to holiday lettings now; either that or Langdale has bred a distinctively lanky kind of person with a fondness for four-wheel drive vehicles and striding about addressing his fellows in loud, confident tones.

Being close to Ambleside, Langdale is popular and often busy, but even in mid-summer any visitor standing at the western end near Stool End, surrounded by grand mountains on all sides and the expanse of the valley before them, cannot fail to have a sense of remoteness, of being somewhere special.

Chapel Stile is the modest village at the entrance to the valley. This clump of trees, apparently growing out of the rock, is in a field by the roadside. Once a centre for quarrying, the old gunpowder works that once served the quarries is now a holiday timeshare site.

Langdale seen from the fells above Chapel Stile; drawn on the spot

Bow Fell

Langdale has some of the best walks in the Lake District, and one of the very best is a long arc at the western end of the valley, over Bow Fell and Crinkle Crags.

This arc can be tackled clockwise or anti-clockwise, as you please, but if you prefer to walk with the sun in your face, then anti-clockwise is best, for once you're on the tops, much of the walk is in a direct line to the south.

From the Stickle Barn Inn, at the bottom of Stickle Ghyll, there is a clear path following a wall behind the Inn, skirting the lower slopes of the fells and passing beneath Raven Crag. As you walk along you might hear disembodied voices emanating from the clear air above; if you do, pause and study the crags for a few minutes, where you'll eventually see rock climbers engaged in their art and sport, shouting or just speaking to each other as they progress up the rocks and crags in their seemingly effortless way. Their voices carry clearly, echoing off the cliff face.

The path continues behind the Old Dungeon Ghyll Hotel, slowly curving around to the north-west until, about a mile past the hotel, it leaves the walled and managed farmland to enter Mickleden proper. The vegetation changes abruptly at the last wall, becoming rougher and wilder as you progress along the deep, wide valley, with the stone-strewn slopes of Langdale Fell on your right tumbling down from the rocky heights of Gimmer Crag and Pike o' Stickle.

Mickleden is an entire lesson in glacial geology. It is perfectly U-shaped, with steep sides that sweep around to its termination beneath Rossett Crag. The Ordnance Survey map confirms its regularity, with the contours traced out in a steady horizontal arc, broken only by Rossett Gill. Towards its end there are mounds of moraine scattered about, dumped by the melting glacier at the end of the last ice age. I sometimes wonder what made the glacier so tidy minded, leaving its debris neatly piled in hummocks rather than chaotically strewn about the valley bottom.

Towards the end of the valley there is a footbridge and a division of paths. On the right is the route up Stake Gill to join Stake Pass and the path to Borrowdale, but our route takes us over the footbridge and along the stone-built path that ascends Rossett Gill. This path, which has been substantially reconstructed, follows the old pony route, dating back to the days when people relied on animals to transport them and their goods from one valley to another. It zig-zags its way up, sometimes to the extent that you might think you're zigging or zagging much too far to the right or left, but keep faith, for it will take you to the top at a steady gradient, emerging at the top of Rossett Gill with the heights of Rossett Pike on your right. There's a grand view from here back down the Gill and into Mickleden, with Pike o' Stickle proudly pointing up to the sky.

The path now drops down to Angle Tarn. This little tarn, shaped like a speech bubble and a favourite spot for rough campers, sits in its corrie with the crags of Hanging Knotts behind it and a valley before it, down which the glacier that once carved out the tarn made its final exit long ago.

There is a choice at Angle Tarn. Just beyond it, as the ground rises again, there is a rough path off to the left that leads up to Ore Gap. It certainly cuts off a corner, but it's in a poor and badly eroded state. The alternative is to keep to the main path for about a mile and a half until you reach another crossing of ways below Esk Hause. There is a very distinctive shelter here: a stone-walled cross, easily recognisable. Even more distinctive is the great dark mass of Great End up in front of you, marking the start of the Scafell range.

However, Great End is not today's destination, so leaving the main route, turn sharp left at the shelter onto a path that rises gently up to the Hause[2]. Another left turn, so you're facing south-east, and there is Esk Pike up in front, where the day's real adventure starts.

Crossing Esk Pike entails some scrambling and a confusion of paths. As is often the case, the main path does not actually take you over the summit but skirts it somewhat on the south-west side; you will have to make a short detour to reach the real top, before dropping down the Pike's gentler south-eastern side to Ore Gap, where the ascent of Bow Fell, one of the Lake District's giants, begins.

In 1698 the aristocratic traveller Celia Fiennes went on a tour of the English Lakes. She kept a journal, in which she described the area, with urbane wit, as 'mostly rocks'. I would guess she formed this opinion without having visited the summit of Bow Fell.

For the top of Bow Fell really is mostly rocks. They lie thickly strewn everywhere, many of them sharp-edged and lying at crazy angles, waiting to

---

[2] At which point it is as well to know what a 'hause' is. A northern dialect word, it refers to a lower connecting ridge between two higher fells. If that is a little difficult to imagine, be assured it is the sort of thing that you recognise immediately once you're there.

trap ankles or cut fingers. Lovers of lunar landscapes will find much to satisfy them here. But when the weather is clear, the views are magnificent, especially of Sca Fell and Scafell Pike, but also far afield across Langdale to the Helvellyn range in the north, and westward out to the sea.

That said, out of maybe seven visits I've made to Bowfell over the last decade or so, at least five of them were in thick mist. Fortunately the ascents and the summit are marked with cairns that loom up out of the white fog to guide you, and so long as you regularly take a compass bearing it's safe. The only likely source of confusion might be as you leave the summit heading south to Crinkle Crags, where the path veers off to the east for a couple of hundred metres, before swinging round again to the south for the descent. The reason for this diversion can be seen clearly and dramatically if you look back from Three Tarns at the bottom. From there you'll see the huge buttressed rocky crags running around the southern face of the fell – not at all somewhere for walkers to be.

The southern face of Bow Fell, seen from Three Tarns

Apart from the dramatic views that present themselves on clear days, Bow Fell has another surprise: Great Slab. As you move off the summit towards Crinkle Crags the slab comes into view just at the point where the path swings south down to Three Tarns. It is exactly what it says: a gigantic flat slab of rock, sloping down towards the valley for some 200 feet.

Crinkle Crags

The descent from Bow Fell leads down to Three Tarns, where there is another crossing of paths and two exit points, should it be necessary to cut the walk short. One leads down over The Band, the great mass of land that sits at the end of Great Langdale. The other makes a bee-line for Oxendale, following Hell Gill.

Three Tarns is a good place to pause, maybe for lunch (so long as you can find shelter from the wind that often howls through here) because it affords many views. Behind, there is Bow Fell; in front Crinkle Crags; on the left Great Langdale and on the right a grand panoramic view of the Sca Fells, with the dramatic gap between Sca Fell and Scafell Pike – one of those iconic and instantly recognisable Lakes scenes – in full view.

Sca Fell, Mickledore and Scafell Pike, seen from Three Tarns

Crinkle Crags is well named. It is a long ridge running north–south, consisting of a sequence of rocky ups and downs, or indeed, Crinkles. Wainwright, who enthused mightily about them, listed five Crinkles. None is particularly high, but the appeal is their roughness, their variety and the views they provide, especially down the gullies leading down the east face.

Looking down Mickle Door, not to be confused with Mickledore, something else entirely (see sketch above)

And then there is Bad Step. Walking from the north, Bad Step is on the fourth crinkle, soon encountered on the scramble down from the peak. The path drops steeply over rock, a route made by the boots of many confident walkers in the past, until it is abruptly halted by a large chock stone above a sudden drop that looks impassable.

Wainwright, who, as already noted, had much to say about Crinkle Crags, wrote that this is the sort of place anyone would get down in a flash if there was a £5 note lying at the bottom. He wrote that in 1959. Allowing for inflation, that is the equivalent of more than £100 in today's money, and I'm still not sure it's enough.

The problem can be seen from the bottom, the view walkers will have if they approach from the south. Looking more like the entrance to an ancient tomb or a leftover from the film-set of *Raiders of the Lost Ark*, Bad Step is a gaping hole, with two large chock stones across the top and steep vertical sides.

Bad Step

Seen from even further back it looks like an open mouth, with loose rocks – actually the spoilage of the footpath – vomiting out down the fellside.

What to do? Reversing our expedition for a few moments, the way *up* is via the rocks on the right-hand side of the mouth. With long legs, this can be done relatively easily: I've watched people do it. But ascent is always easier than descent, and although while coming down it's possible to make some progress, you inevitably reach a drop that is just a little too much. Holding on to the rockface, you find that there is no place for your foot to go next, while the bottom lies a foot or two further down. So you hang on there thinking, well, all I have to do is make a backwards leap down and I'll be fine, but the bottom is anything but level or stable, and the risk of a nasty fall outweighs the benefit of any fictional £100 by some margin. Retreat is the only answer.

Apart from injured pride, there is no harm in this. There is another route that swings around to the west of the Crinkle, skirting it more or less entirely, and this will bring you round to the bottom of the Bad Step where you can sit and watch others going through the same frustrating experience.

As on Esk Pike, the main path often avoids the summits of the Crinkles, preferring to stay on the west side, away from the precipitous cliffs over Oxendale. However, there are many tracks and ghost paths criss-crossing the area, and in bad weather it can be confusing. On one expedition in heavy mist, thinking we knew the route well, a small group of us strode confidently but blindly along the path until someone had the sense to check with a compass and discovered we were energetically proceeding north; somehow we had made a 180-degree turn. I still do not know how that happened.

Once the last Crinkle is passed, things become easier. There is a long, broad path down to Red Tarn – or at least close to it – and then another path, mostly rebuilt with stones, that skirts around the western flank of Pike o' Blisco all the way down to a footbridge in Oxendale, and from there to Stool End Farm and the track back to the start.

Waterfall cascade seen from the path around Pike o' Blisco

Looking back from the Pike o' Blisco path, the Crinkles can be seen peeping over the edge

Pike o' Blisco

It's labelled Pike of Blisco on the Ordnance Survey maps, but is known as Pike o' Blisco by all its friends.

Standing on its own, towering over Oxendale, this is one of those mountains that is instantly recognisable because of its distinctive shape: a near-perfect cone, topped by a strangely corkscrewed set of rock terraces twisting around the summit that make the last few dozen metres of ascent something of an enjoyable challenge.

Pike o' Blisco, seen from The Band

I neglected Pike o' Blisco in the past, mainly because it isn't easily linked into a long ridge walk. After Esk Pike, Bow Fell and Crinkle Crags, it's usually just a bit too much and too late in the day to take in Pike o' Blisco too, but it can be included in a shorter circuit of, say, Crinkle Crags and The Band, starting from the Blea Tarn road that links Great and Little Langdales. On its own, it makes a great afternoon's walk if time is limited.

If even that is too much, an easy and direct way of tackling Pike o' Blisco is to start not in Langdale but from Wrynose Pass; there's even a small parking area near the Three Shire Stone to start out from. Being a popular route the path is pretty obvious, leading in the direction of Red Tarn, then turning off to the right a little way before the tarn is reached, up the Pike's flank.

There are two summits to Pike o' Blisco, connected by peat and a stone platform that has had some repairs done to it, so heavy is the pedestrian traffic. Many years ago the summit cairn was a tall pillar (that is how Wainwright drew it) but that went long ago, and the modern cairn is a more modest affair. The corkscrew effect seen from The Band is quite evident close up, and although the path from Wrynose does not approach from the rockiest side, there is still scope for some exploratory scrambling.

On the way back down to Wrynose Pass it's worth seeking out a little curiosity described by Wainwright, possibly even discovered by him (he proudly believed, perhaps tongue-in-cheek, that this honour was his) on Black Crag: a free-standing rock needle, precariously balanced on a rock plinth. He drew it and described it, but did not give its location in much detail, and when I went looking for it I spent much time scrambling over and around the crag – which is a fairly large affair – only to find that all my trouble was unnecessary, because the needle is easily visible from the main path as it skirts the base of crag.

Wainwright's Needle, on Black Crag

The needle stands some 20 feet high and is quite separate from the surrounding rock, balanced on its blunt end. Equally curious are the marks like cannon-ball indentations in the face of the rock all around. Roughly circular and about nine inches in diameter, they are brown inside, contrasting with the blue-grey of the rock, and something of an enigma.

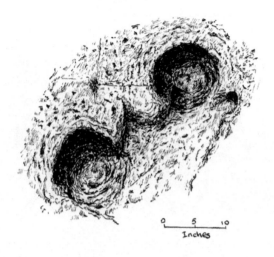

These indentations on Black Crag look like they were made by cannon balls, but presumably they are a consequence of the volcanic origins of these rocks; volcanic bombs, perhaps.

Pavey Ark

Possibly the most popular path in the whole of Langdale is the gasping slog up Stickle Ghyll to Stickle Tarn, at the foot of Pavey Ark.

At the bottom of Stickle Ghyll is the Stickle Barn Inn. A few years ago it looked cheerily incongruous, with strings of gaudy lights outside and loud music on Saturday nights that attracted large crowds from far away. More recently it seems to have sobered up, but it still offers good beer and food, with a paved terrace outside where you can sit out late on warm summer evenings to enjoy the comfortable feeling that goes with a good meal, good beer, good company, and the glorious surroundings of the Langdale valley as swallows swoop past the tables and the golden sun slowly sets.

But it's not evening yet; we are only just setting out. The main path runs round the rear of the pub, and is clearly signposted. The ascent begins on the left side of the Ghyll, but soon comes to a bridge offering a choice: cross over to the right side or continue on the left. The right-hand side is where the newly built path lies; on the left the old path continues but quickly degenerates into an eroded mess. There is a second crossing point a little further on, but without a bridge, and in the interests of dry feet and of avoiding further damage to the old path, the best advice is to keep to the right-hand side.

Fallen tree in Stickle Ghyll

The going is moderately steep, but the path is solidly built and helps you along. As the gradient levels off, you cross the Ghyll again by way of some enormous stepping stones – although 'leaping boulders' might convey their scale more accurately. You then rise up to the tarn, with the dark mass of Pavey Ark hanging overhead.

Pavey Ark and Stickle Tarn

Stickle Tarn was dammed in the early 19th century to provide water to the small community below, and there is a low wall across the edge of the tarn where one can sit while considering what to do next. If the intention is to climb Pavey Ark, there are at least four alternatives available. The first is to the left, an obvious path that works its way up between Harrison Stickle and the Ark. It may be obvious, but it's a slog, better kept in mind as a quick exit route from the top than as an ascent. The other three all begin towards the far end of the tarn, and can be approached by moving clockwise or anti-clockwise around the water. Anti-clockwise is slightly longer, but you will be treated to a dramatic view of Pavey Ark, its grim, vertical rock face looming above the tarn. Unfortunately, to get there you have to cross the Ghyll again, which is now the outflow from the tarn, and this is harder than you might think if you like to keep your boots dry. There are stepping stones, but they're downstream a little way and not all that obvious or helpful.

Of these other three routes, the easiest is the North Rake, which can't be seen from the dam but lies just around the north-east edge of the Ark's face, leading up a sort of rock alleyway to the summit. Wainwright described it as being on grass, and while the grass has long been trampled away, and several sections involve hand and toe scrambles up rock ladders, it's safe and enjoyable, and provides another reliable route back down in bad weather.

The two classic routes – both of them daring and exhilarating – are Jack's Rake and Easy Gully. Conveniently, they begin at the same point, so you have the opportunity to sit and contemplate them both before making your choice, always remembering that the North Rake is available if they look too daunting. The entry point is quite high up the slopes of the mountainside, at the lower boundary of the rock face, and reached by a scramble over rough rock-strewn ground.

Easy Gully

Easy Gully was surely named in irony. It is indeed a gully, as can clearly be seen when it comes into view if you approach it walking clockwise around the tarn. From the point where Jack's Rake and Easy Gully meet, the gully lies to the right, rising vertically up a deep cleft in the rocks. No, there is no doubt about its qualifications as a gully; the irony lies in the term 'Easy'.

Easy Gully: it's a matter of opinion

The ascent starts easily enough. It's steep, with lots of loose rocks, and it suffers from the effects of many boots trampling over it, but that is not unusual. Eventually you reach a large rock jutting out like a canopy, perfectly positioned by the mountain gods to provide protection against the rain. The way gets a little steeper after that, until you reach a point where the gully is blocked by a tumbled mass of boulders. This is where things get interesting.

You find yourself facing another large, overhanging rock that seems to want to nudge you away backwards, down the slope behind, which is now steep enough to demand some mental concentration. To the left there is an arrangement something like in the sketch below. (This was drawn later from memory, so I can't vouch for its physical accuracy, but its subjective accuracy is precise. Drawing wasn't uppermost in my mind when I was there...)

The boulder blockage in Easy Gully

Clinging on while considering the next move, it seems that you have to haul yourself over the lower boulder on the left, but it's not obvious where the hand-holds are, and it slopes down precipitously without any footholds. Worse, even a small backpack will surely become wedged under the overhanging rock above.

But there's no need to panic, for there is an alternative on the right that looks like a manageable climb up a narrow passage – but it's impossible to see what lies only a few metres further on, and retreat looks tricky.

It is what might be called a trilemma: to go right, left, or admit defeat and descend. Each walker will have to make the choice that is right for them, which is, indeed, what I did.

Jack's Rake

The fourth route is the famous Jack's Rake. This rises diagonally across the face of the cliff, and you can see it clearly from the opposite side of the tarn. It is where fell-walking and rock climbing meet: a demanding climb for walkers, an easy walk for climbers. It's the closest a Lake District walker is likely to get to rock climbing, and is magnificent, exhilarating and hair-raising in equal measure.

The start of Jack's Rake

To get to the start you have to climb the slopes above the tarn as far as the base of the crags. The rake's start is obvious, a sort of staircase rising across the face of the cliff, with a vertical wall to the right and a little parapet on the left. This parapet is useful in a practical and psychological sense: practical because it provides footholds that assist your climb, and psychological because it helps take your mind off the drop to the tarn below. This comforting little wall continues for much of the ascent, helping prevent your imagination from dwelling too much on the multiple ways your expedition could come to an abrupt end. There are only a couple of places where it forgoes its role as protector – gaps where you're left looking down the abyss, if you're bold enough to look – and some courage is required. The climb demands the use of fingers and toes all the way, with one or two knee-trembler moments when, with hands and feet all fully engaged in holding on to the rock face, you find that the next move requires an impossible juxtaposition of limbs in order to haul yourself up a few more inches. Things continue in this way until eventually the gradient levels off, and suddenly you can walk upright again and make your way over the scattered rocks and grass to the summit.

Wainwright mentioned using Jack's Rake as a means of descent, an idea that seems a little crazy. Even finding the entry point from the top is no easy task, with severe consequences if you get it wrong, but in fairness he was not really advocating its use. It has to be said that the rake is hard for a walker, and requires a degree of skill and nerve. I'd recommend not going alone – company can help sustain confidence – and certainly not attempting it in wet or poor weather when it can be genuinely dangerous.

The summit is wild, with tumbled rocks everywhere. Once reached, you can spend an enjoyable hour or two exploring the summits of Harrison Stickle and Pike o' Stickle, the elongated dome of which stands guard high over Mickleden. The great line of crags arching round from Pavey Ark to Pike o' Stickle, towering high over Langdale and Mickleden, is great walking territory, but the landscape just beyond it, to the north and west, is dull. It's criss-crossed with paths, including, a mile or two northwards, the pedestrian highway on Greenup Edge. But these are paths to get you from one place to another, not paths to tread for their own sake.

There are at least two paths back down from Harrison that more or less follow Dungeon Ghyll. If you take the clear path west off the Pike, with Pike o' Stickle in front of you, you will drop down to a crossing of paths; turn left, following the contours, with Loft Crag ahead of you, until you reach the head of Dungeon Ghyll. If you cross it you'll join a long path that curves under Loft Crag and then out above Raven Crag and eventually down to the bottom of Stickle Ghyll. However, the views of the Ghyll and its waterfalls are better from the alternative (and shorter) path that keeps to the Harrison side. From here you get splendid views down into the gully, which rapidly and steeply falls away on your right-hand side. The path takes a fairly direct line, then curves right, under Pike How, and down to Stickle Ghyll. My only grumble is that this is a constructed path, built with its flat stone surfaces sloping down, so in wet weather (ie 'normal' weather) the descent can be slippery and hard work.

But even on this path you're liable to miss Dungeon Ghyll Force. After countless visits to Langdale over many years I failed to see it until recently. It's marked on the Ordnance Survey map, but in a half-hearted sort of way, and you really have to hunt about for it, scrambling down steep muddy embankments and splashing through water. I got there after heavy rain, and the only way to see the falls was from a position standing in twelve inches of fast-flowing water that quickly filled my boots: it's an exploration best done at the end of a day's walk rather than the start.

Wordsworth knew this spot and wrote about it:

Into a chasm a mighty block
Hath fallen, and made a bridge of rock:
The gulf is deep below;
And, in a basin black and small,
Receives a lofty waterfall.

His description is concise and accurate.

Dungeon Ghyll Force

Pike o' Stickle

Its distinctive shape means Pike o' Stickle is easily recognised from many angles, even at a distance. From the front it is tall and bold, with straight slopes screaming down into Mickleden and a distinctive rounded summit pointing to the sky. There's a steep scree run down its side that once had a crooked sign at the top asking you not to run down it. Wise advice, but in fact these screes are the site of an axe factory, dating back to the Stone Age. Large numbers of stone axes – some apparently dumped as sub-standard – have been found here, while examples found elsewhere in the country can be traced back to their Langdale origins. They were made of Greenstone, which occurs in a narrow band on the heights of the Pike. One can only wonder at how people so long ago came to find the stone up here in such an inaccessible place, and at the scale of the industry they seem to have established, clinging to the fellside.

Pike o' Stickle: Don't Run Down the Scree

In a way Pike o' Stickle puts me in mind of an Italian church. From the front it's all grandeur and splendour, but from behind you can see that the facade is a stick-on job, covering a much duller and rather disappointing rear. If you don't believe me, here is a comparison.

Rear view of Pike o' Stickle

Rear view of San Giovanni del Nulla

3 BORROWDALE

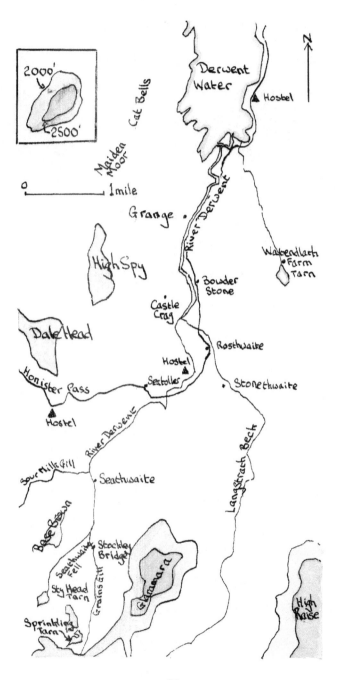

Borrowdale viewed across Derwent Water

Five thousand years ago the Lake District was almost entirely covered by forest. Where we now see sheep-nibbled fells of grass and rock, there were once huge forests of oak and elm filling the valleys and climbing up the mountainsides to a height of 2,000 feet. The great change came with the arrival of people, who began the slow but inexorable process of clearing the trees as they expanded their territory to establish farms and settlements. Their work was substantially completed a long time ago: long before the felling of the oak forests in the south of England to build ships, long before the arrival of the Vikings or the Saxons before them, and long before the Romans who came and built their forts and roads and walls. Most of the original forests on the high ground were gone by about 1,000BC.

To a modern visitor, this seems hard to understand or believe. The fells are beautiful, but the soil covering them is poor and thin, and it's hard to see how it could have sustained forests. And how could these people, equipped with what must have been primitive tools, have achieved such a change – even if it took them a couple of millennia to do it? For that matter, why did they bother at all, for the mountains must have been dangerous, inhospitable places and surely there were richer and easier pickings elsewhere?

They weren't looking for timber. This was no doubt a useful asset, but what they really wanted was land, and land high up on the fells was habitable because the weather was evidently warmer then. And while their tools were indeed primitive, they were extremely effective. First, they had stone axes, often made locally, such as at the 'factory' on Pike o' Stickle in Langdale. Next was fire, which could be used just as now in tropical rainforests to clear large areas rapidly and indiscriminately. But they had other weapons, perhaps their most effective of all: teeth and hooves. The teeth and hooves, that is, of their animals – probably cattle and swine in the early days, followed much later by the king of the grazers, the sheep. For sheep are dogged and relentless, eating virtually anything green[3], and wherever they roam no sapling or young plant stands a chance of growing. Grazing land was what those early settlers wanted, and as they cleared small areas by axe and fire, their animals prevented any regeneration of the original forest cover. In time the cleared soil was leached by the rain so that it degenerated to the point where, even if the settlers had packed up and left, the forests would not have recovered, at least not in their original form.

So the Lake District we see now may look natural, but it is in many ways a landscape shaped by men and their animals. The sheep are still there of course, endlessly nibbling away at the grass and any hapless young plants rash enough to show their heads above the surface. During the foot-and-mouth epidemic of 2001 much was said about the devastating effect the permanent loss of the Herdwick sheep would have on the appearance of the fells, but the Herdwicks survived and the panic is over for the time being. One day they may disappear, either because of disease or more probably because of economics, for hill farming is a hard business with low profit margins and a declining number of young people who want to take it up[4]. If the sheep were ever to go, the whole character of the Lake District would change once again. What the outcome would be is hard to guess, but it won't be a return to those mountainous forests of oak and elm.

Except, perhaps, in Borrowdale[5]. For Borrowdale is one place where it's possible to get a glimpse of what the Lake District might have looked like five thousand years ago. Immediately south of Derwent Water there is a wide floodplain criss-crossed by walls and a few paths; it is a functioning floodplain, and sometimes after heavy rain is completely

---

[3] But not daffodils, which might account for the famous display of dancing yellow daffodils eulogised by Wordsworth.

[4] Or who can afford anywhere to live.

[5] Or maybe Ennerdale: see page 73.

impassable. Further south is the little settlement of Grange, and it is here, at the 'Jaws of Borrowdale' that the ancient wooded character of the lakes can be sensed. This is a pinch-point, where the Borrowdale valley narrows, squeezed between crags on either side, and the forest extends gloriously all around, rising steeply up the rock faces. The trees are predominantly of the older species, with much oak, although they have been substantially replanted by man. You can't really see them to the best effect from the road, which in the early morning is heavily trafficked by people hurrying by to get a parking space down at Seathwaite, so you have to use your feet.

I'd say one of the most startling views to be had in the Lakes, out of many, is on the path that runs from Grange southwards to Castle Crag. It starts unexceptionally, but very prettily, passing some campsites and then entering the woods, until it abruptly reaches a point where the river Derwent widens in a huge bend with trees all around and wooded slopes rising in the background. It seems Amazonian rather than Cumbrian, and is quite unexpected, stopping me dead in my tracks the first time I saw it.

The River Derwent, or the Amazon?

Castle Crag

With its height not quite reaching 1,000 feet, Castle Crag doesn't have much by way of statistical qualification as a mountain, but it makes up for its lack of stature in other ways. Even Wainwright was so impressed that he gave it eight pages in the *North Western Fells*.

Castle Crag

Castle Crag stands at the Jaws of Borrowdale, an obstruction in the throat of the valley, conical, with steeply wooded, craggy sides. Its steepness is perfectly obvious from a distance, so it should come as no surprise to find the ascent quite demanding – although it always does.

Walking south from Grange, just past the Amazonian view over the Derwent, the path forks. The right-hand path soon becomes a broad rocky track leading to the western side of Castle Crag. Take a left turn onto a fairly obvious path and you soon find yourself huffing and puffing up the steep slopes to cross a stone wall, where you will arrive at the foot of a huge mound of quarry spoil. For Castle Crag has been quarried and hacked and burrowed into for centuries, somehow retaining its dignity throughout.

The path zig-zags its way up the enormous slopes of the spoil heap until it levels off and divides. Go right up a small ascent, passing under a tree (possibly stumbling over its exposed roots), and the summit is soon reached: a roughly circular domain with a rocky hump in the middle that has a war memorial set into it. There is said to have once been an ancient fort up here, and while it's easy to see that this would have been an easily defended location and an excellent look-out point, there is no trace of it now, at least not to an untrained eye. Besides, a large part of the summit isn't even there any more, having being quarried out. To see this, return to the point where the path divided and go the other way. It leads into a bizarre little landscape, the surface strewn with quarry spoilage, the path curving round into an enclosed rock amphitheatre hacked into the fell-top: the quarry. But this isn't what makes the scenery bizarre; it's all the standing stones. Dozens, hundreds of them. Visitors have taken to standing the long flat slabs of quarry waste up on end, so the impression is of being in a fantastical graveyard. It's an eerie experience being there alone in the echoing chamber of the quarry, surrounded by row after row of standing stones.

The standing stones on Castle Crag

These rocks were precariously but impressively balanced on top of one of the standing stones

Having tired of the quarry, it's time to consider the descent. One could of course retrace one's steps down the spoil heap, but there is another path that leads off to the east, down to Rosthwaite. Or, there are at least two such paths, the correct one and the one I once took. Looking for the Rosthwaite descent, I soon found a path that veered off to the left down the spoil slopes. The bouquet of flowers at the top should have given me pause, but I went on and soon found myself on a rough path over loose boulders and rubble, twisting and turning steeply down the slope. Nothing seemed stable, and pausing at one point I realised that I had hundreds of tons of steeply heaped rocks directly above me on one hand, and a precipitous drop over more shifting rocks on the other. This was not a comfortable situation, made even more surprising because it came on me so quickly, within moments of leaving the top.

However, no harm was done and I reached the woods below the rocks and walked through the trees down to the riverside path, where I soon saw the correct path, rising quite clearly over the grass into the trees. If you're unfamiliar with the top of Castle Crag, choose your exit carefully.

The path to Rosthwaite follows the Derwent, at this point a pretty but less grand flow than it becomes half a mile downstream. It was early summer when the Castle Crag adventure occurred, and all along the river there were swallows, house martins and swifts, all three species together, swooping through the air and calling out, each in their own distinctive way, as they feasted on insects.

Borrowdale Youth Hostel has a board hung on the wall recording time trials from the door of the hostel to the top of Castle Crag. They ranged (in summer 2013) from an impressive 11 minutes and 39 seconds to 20 minutes 15 seconds, with one other coming in at 75 minutes – but this brave contender was only seven years old.

The Bowder Stone

The Bowder Stone

This oddity lies on the east side of Borrowdale's jaws. There is a track leading up to it from the road. Said to weigh 2,000 tons and standing 30 feet high, it isn't just its bulk that impresses – although it does – but the way it stands so audaciously balanced on its pointed lower end. That is how it appears from one angle, but really it rests on its lower edge, like the keel of a ship, a balancing trick it has performed for 10,000 years or more.

There are at least two theories about how the Bowder Stone got here. One states that the stone is a visitor from Scotland, having travelled down on a glacier, inch by inch, to be gently lowered into this position as the ice melted thousands of years ago. This is certainly an imaginative and attention-grabbing idea, and not entirely fanciful because there are indeed stones in England that were transported from Scotland by the ice. The other theory takes a more grounded position, you might say, observing that the stone is made of the same type of rock as the rest of Borrowdale, so it most probably fell from the crags above in what must have been a noisy and destructive event (not that anyone was there to witness it).

The 2,000-ton claim also looks shaky. In the early nineteenth century a local gent called Joseph Pocklington recognised the money-making potential of the stone and turned it into a tourist attraction, putting a ladder up against it so that visitors could climb to the top (for a charge) and building a hermitage next to it, along with a druid stone, to augment the air of ancient mystery. He estimated the rock's weight as 1,771 tons, a figure that was rounded up to a more memorable 2,000 tons in the guidebooks. However, a local geologist, Alan Smith, has more recently estimated its weight to be merely 1,294 tons, which is still one very big boulder. It was Mr Smith who pointed out that the stone is geologically identical to the crags above it, and that for a Scottish glacier to have carried it here, it would have had to travel *up* Borrowdale, in the wrong direction.

There is still a viewing ladder allowing you to climb to the top – without charge – while more adventurous souls can sometimes be seen climbing the rock, without ropes but with mattresses strewn on the ground below them, white streaks of chalk dust marking their handholds in the stone.

Pocklington seems to have been quite a character. Apart from the hermitage he also built Bowderstone Cottage next to the stone, and installed an old woman there to greet visitors and take payment. The cottage was still occupied by custodians of the stone until well into the 20th century, and is still there now, used as a climbers' hut. It was Pocklington who built a large house for himself on the shores of Derwent Water, named Barrow House, now the Derwent Water Youth Hostel. He even constructed a picturesque waterfall at the rear of the house, still to be seen today.

South of the constriction at Castle Crag, Borrowdale opens out again in the classic Lake District manner, with a broad, flat-bottomed valley criss-crossed by stone walls and surrounded by rising fells. This is the valley of the Thwaites. Rosthwaite, Seathwaite and Stonethwaite are the best known, but then there is Longthwaite, Burthwaite and Thorneywaite – six of them, clustered together in a small area. The suffix, which means meadow, tells of the Viking origins of these settlements – or perhaps the Vikings' seizure and renaming of them[6].

---

[6] In his guide to the Northern Fells Wainwright recommended finding all the

From Rosthwaite there's a pleasant walk over the River Derwent and past Borrowdale Youth Hostel, rising into some trees to emerge at Seatoller and the road that veers off up to Honister Hause and the slate mine.

The slate mine is still active, but there was once a very different mining industry here. Maybe five hundred years ago, shepherds found some soft, black material lying on the surface of Seathwaite Fell. Thinking it was coal they tried to burn it, but it resisted. On the other hand it was good for marking their sheep, and local people soon realised it was perfect for writing and drawing. Its fame quickly spread: they had found graphite, and graphite of very high quality. Pencils were first made with Cumbrian graphite in Elizabethan times, and demand for this special material grew so much that by the 18th century it was valuable enough for soldiers to be posted at the Seathwaite mines to stop people stealing it.

Sadly these security measures weren't imposed because of massive demand from artists desperate for high-quality graphite pencils to draw with. No, the truth was stranger still, because the graphite was used primarily to line moulds for making cannon balls. Hence the government's interest and the decision to post armed guards. However, graphite *was* in demand for drawing, and Cumbrian graphite was highly prized and exported widely; it's likely the Italian artists of the Renaissance used it during the 16th century. A pencil factory was established at Keswick and it had a near monopoly until a Frenchman, Nicolas-Jacques Conté, invented a way of making pencils using inferior quality graphite by grinding it up with clay and baking it: the Conté crayon.

By the late 19th century the mines were worked out and they closed, but the pencil factory continued. It is of course where the

Thwaites on the OS one-inch map of the Lake District as a way of filling in time on a rainy day. He said there were 81 of them (see his chapter on Blencathra, page 31). At least one blogger on the internet, 'Scriptor Senex', has located them all, and provided a list. He claims there are even more on the 2.5 inch maps.

Derwent brand of pencils and artists' materials originated. Ironically, the factory long ago adopted the Conté manufacturing process that had once undermined its position, and it became an important employer in Keswick. However, by the beginning of the 21st century the factory had become outdated and the company wanted to replace it with a more modern plant. Their plans were supported by the staff, local people and the council, but the National Park rejected them. Unable to reach agreement, it looked for a while like the factory would go the way of so many others and move to China. Yet it did not. A new factory was built near Workington, only a few miles away but outside the National Park, and all operations moved there where they continue successfully today. The National Park meanwhile is left with the decaying hulk of an abandoned factory in Keswick.

The oddly named Base Brown

The road to Seathwaite Farm continues along a narrowing flat-bottomed valley with the oddly named Base Brown on one side, looking like a giant has leaned on it too hard and pushed it out of shape, and Glaramara on the other. The lonely farm is at the end of the road, but its isolation is only intermittent, because the road is usually lined with the parked cars that bring crowds of walkers who hurry through the farm yard and set off towards Stockley Bridge and path leading to the great fells of the central area: Great Gable, Scafell Pike, Great End and all their neighbours.

Seathwaite Farm and Sourmilk Gill

The path to Stockley Bridge is built with stone and heavily trod, following our old friend the River Derwent upstream to its origin, the point where Styhead Gill and Grains Gill meet. The bridge is an arched stone construction, built in the old Cumbrian style at a point where the Gill tumbles down a little rocky gorge into a deep pool.

Stockley Bridge

Just over the bridge there is a choice of paths. The one straight ahead follows Grains Gill in a direct line to Great End and Sprinkling Tarn, while the one to the right leads to Styhead Tarn and the Corridor Route to the Scafells. Those who fancy an exhilarating walk among the high mountains without necessarily climbing any of them – not a bad option when the cloud is low – might go right, to make a little circuit beneath Great Gable and Great End, taking in both tarns and returning via the Grains Gill path. However, both paths lead out of this Chapter and into Chapter 9, so these are matters to be returned to later.

Glaramara

This curiously named fell offers an attractive route back down to Borrowdale from the high central fells, a route that seems to be much less used than the paths along Grains Gill or Styhead Gill. It also offers a series of grand views extending for many miles in clear weather, including a reverse view of the Langdales to the right – particularly of Pike o' Stickle – and Great Gable, dark and ominous on the left. A little further north there's a great side-view of the sheer cliffs of Honister Crag.

Fleetwith Pike and Honister Crag seen from Glaramara

For all that, the highlight must be the view ahead, along Borrowdale and over Derwent Water to Skiddaw's hazy silhouette in the distance. This is the view that makes all the day's efforts worthwhile.

Derwent Water and Skiddaw, seen from Glaramara

It seems that in comparison with its neighbouring fells, Glaramara is neglected by walkers. On a sunny summer's day, with large numbers of people hurrying back and forth along the Corridor Route and the Styhead-Sprinkling-Angle Tarn superhighway, I saw no more than half a dozen walkers up on Glaramara, most of them hurrying back down to Borrowdale. It's true that Glaramara isn't so exciting in its own right – although there is a short sharp crag face to descend from the summit that can take you by surprise[7] – but it's worth the effort, and will take you away from the crowds even at busy times.

The fells and valley north of Glaramara. This was drawn on the spot, blots and all, on the path to Seatoller, near Glaramara Outdoors Centre. I was sitting so still as I drew that a red squirrel ran past my feet.

---

[7] It certainly surprised me, and having got to the bottom with some use of my own derrière, I found I'd lost my wallet from my back pocket and had to climb nearly all the way back up again to find it.

Watendlath Farm is on the fells above Borrowdale, to the east. Accessible by road, it has a tea shop and a trout fishing lake, and is a popular draw for walkers and drivers alike. It is picturesque, and much photographed, so instead of yet another picture of the farm, here is a view looking northwards up the valley that leads to it. Sketching did not last long: I was plagued by ravenous midges.

This yew tree, next to the path, has squeezed its way up between two rocks, like toothpaste from a tube

Roughly speaking, this is the area bounded by Borrowdale, Derwent Water and Bassenthwaite to the east, and Ennerdale to the south. It includes the fells around Buttermere, and even, since categories here are somewhat arbitrary, Pillar and Steeple. However, the largest area is where the true North West fells lie, a group of long lumpy ridges fanning out from a focal point in the Derwent valley, just north of Keswick: the wonderful Cat Bells, Maiden Moor and High Spy; Causey Pike, with its distinctively sharp-edged profile and knobbly peak, leading to Sail and the rocky heights of Grasmoor; then Grisedale Pike, Hobcarton Crags and Whiteside.

Each ridge provides excellent walking, but not circular high-level walks, so on the return leg you have to retrace your steps or drop down to one of the valleys – or, in the case of Cat Bells, follow the lakeside. Grasmoor offers the possibility of using the bus service between Buttermere and Keswick to complete a circle.

Grisedale Pike

There is a path up Grisedale Pike that starts just outside Braithwaite, off the road leading to the Whinlatter Pass. It's one of those long, slow progressions of a path, tiring, but with no especially difficult sections to blame for your fatigue. The views gradually open out as you rise, the best being to the left over the wide Coledale valley – although you might have to leave the path for a few hundred feet across the hummocky grass to see the valley's termination at Force Crag, with Eel Crag and Grasmoor high above.

The view of Coledale Valley from the path up Grisedale Pike

The summit is narrow, stony and windswept, with a small cairn, but it overlooks the next stage of the walk which now becomes immediately clear, calling you onwards, onwards, to Hobcarton Crag, a great screen of crags rising and falling in a long, flexing, wave, with a clearly visible path all along the top. Who could resist?

Hobcarton Crags seen from Grisedale Pike

The way to it is dead straight down the slope, following the line of a wall, completely collapsed now, but whose white stones are still tidily laid out. Hobcarton Crag's intimidating physicality becomes ever more imposing as you approach, its curtain of rock falling vertically for 500 feet or more, followed by a second drop, almost as great, down a slope of scree all the way to the valley floor.

The walk along its edge is easy enough, but worth taking time over, pausing to look down the cavernous drop on the right. At the far western end the path rises up to Hopegill Head, a rocky, blustery viewpoint, somewhere to forget about daily cares for a while as you struggle to stand upright against the buffeting[8] winds.

The ridge path continues westward towards Whiteside, with spectacularly steep drops into great U-shaped valleys on either side. This ridge walk to

---

[8] The wind plays strange games up here. It is possible to find yourself standing in a pocket of calm, screened from the wind's blasts by towering rocks, while less than fifteen feet away the very grass seems on the point of being torn out of the ground by its roots.

Whiteside is especially good; rough and rocky but not dangerous, with the wild emptiness of the Hope Gill valley on the right, and the Gasgale Crags on the left, falling, in a mirror image of Hobcarton Crags, some 500 feet down to the valley below. The crags aren't easily seen from the path, and the best views have to wait until you reach the end of Whiteside, descending a little and looking back.

Gasgale Crags seen from Whiteside

There is something of the Wild West about the scene. The rocks are heavily laminated, their layers tilted to expose their jagged edges to the sky, with ragged pillars and towers jutting out of the cliff face. Some pockets of dry vegetation cling on in places – in reality heather, but in the imagination, desert scrub. Gullies with dried-up creeks cut down the crag face while in the valley far below Liza Beck can just be glimpsed.

This is a section of the path at the top of Whiteside. It looks like it was made from terracotta, which in a way it was, because these are ancient sedimentary rocks, laid down under a lost sea, baked and compressed and then thrust up to the top of the mountain. The brown, curving layers are badly broken up but very striking. It seems strange that this ancient, eloquent lesson in geology is trampled over daily as a footpath; is it not worth protecting?

Setting aside this Clint Eastwood fantasy, you also get a good view of Crummock Water from here. The sight caught me by surprise when I first came to this spot and for a moment I didn't recognise the lake. Sometimes when you move from one valley after two or three hours of hard walking, and another breaks into view, there's a sense of a shift, of leaving one enclosed little world to enter another, and this was one such occasion, the experience heightened by momentary uncertainty about what I was looking at.

There is no safe route down Gasgale Crags for walkers, but returning to Hopegill Head, there is a broad path curving down to Coledale Hause.

Making my way down here once, I watched a very elderly walker slowly moving towards me. Tall and lean, but stooped, he had a long walking pole in each hand and looked like a creature from a Hollywood sci-fi film, creeping along, slowly and uncertainly, on four spindly legs. When we met I said hello. His attention was fixed on the ground before him, and he slowly and stiffly turned his face to look at me with pale blue eyes, then said something in an East European language that I didn't understand. With that we passed each other by. There are no really easy routes to that remote spot and I wondered how he had got there, and how he would get away later, moving so slowly. It was early afternoon and I was starting to descend, but he was still on the way up.

From Coledale Hause there is a clear rock path down to the Coledale valley, passing through a landscape that duplicates itself as you descend. First it skirts a level, boggy area walled with crags and the ruins of old mine buildings with fanned-out cones of spoil spilling out below them. There's a melancholic feel to the place, a feeling that often attaches to sombre landscapes haunted by the memories of long-gone human activity. This is High Force: interesting enough in itself but no more than the prelude to what comes next, its larger, grander replication further down the valley: Force Crag.

The great craggy screen of Force Crag

Force Crag is an extraordinary sight, a winged barrier of rock straddling the head of Coledale from one side to the other, vertical, rocky, partially wooded, with a pencil-thin waterfall tumbling down its face. It puts me in mind of a giant altar screen high up across the valley. Much of its impact comes from its strange symmetry, with a peak at each end and a dip in the middle, like a Batman emblem, and the waterfall, High Force, running through the dip.

The path sweeps around the southern end of the crag before sloping down to the valley floor. Rusting and derelict mine buildings can be seen tucked away beneath the crag, but while High Force is completely abandoned, down here there is some new activity. Two newly built rectangular pools – not shown on the OS map – lie shining blue in the afternoon sunshine; next to them, notice boards tell the site's story.

The mine first operated in 1835, producing lead, zinc and (a new one to me) barytes, an inert mineral used widely in industry. The National Trust acquired the mine in 1979, and it continued to operate up until 1991 when it closed for good: the last working mineral mine in the Lake District was gone.

The old mine buildings at Force Crag

Unfortunately this silent, closed mine left a persistent and dangerous legacy. Force Crag mine was found to be leaking a toxic mix of heavy metals into Coledale Beck: the helpful notice boards list zinc, cadmium, lead and copper. The new pools are part of a filtration system built by the National Trust in an attempt to remove the toxic metals and clean up the beck. They are fenced off, and visitors are warned about deep water and toxic mud. The sickly looking brown heaps by the pools emit a foul sulphurous smell that lingers in the nostrils even after leaving the place.

The path along the valley bottom back to Braithwaite isn't really a path at all, it's a road, built to serve the mine. A little below, Coledale Beck trickles along.

It's fenced off, but it's easy to see that the rocks standing out above the water are oddly coloured in reddish browns and yellows, each rock painted in a band that ends a few inches above the water surface. Knowing what the source of that colouring might be was not, for once, a source of pleasure.

Causey Pike to Grasmoor

Skiddaw, Great Gable, Pike o' Stickle, Mickledore: they are all mountains (or, in Mickledore's case a link between mountains) that are instantly recognisable from afar, and which provide comforting reference points in moments of uncertainty. Causey Pike is another. Lying on one of the North West's long bumpy ridges, its shape is unmistakable: thin and elongated, its distinctive summit topped with a large knobble of rock that looks unstable, perched on the narrow base of the fell.

Causey Pike seen from the Newlands Valley

A direct and rewarding route is to go straight up the ridge from Stoneycroft, near Stair in the Newlands valley, just past the little bridge over Stoneycroft Gill. The most used path, judging by its condition, climbs the

51

gradient slowly, keeping to the northern flank of the ridge. But there's a more direct way, more or less straight up through the heather and bracken past Ellas Crag to the first named top on the ridge, Rowling End. If in doubt, head for the lone tree standing out on the skyline directly above.

The lone tree on Rowling End

From here the route is obvious, and on a clear day the views are magnificent in all directions. The going is easy until the summit is reached and you encounter that rock knob, which turns out to be quite demanding, requiring the use of hands and feet to conquer it. There are several mini-summits to cross before a sudden descent down to Scar Crags, which provide a long and enjoyable ridge walk with a craggy drop on the left, into the impressively deep and steep-sided Rigg Beck valley.

Newlands Valley seen from Causey Pike

In due course the path descends from Scar Crags, bringing into view possibly the strangest sight in all of the Lake District: the path up Sail.

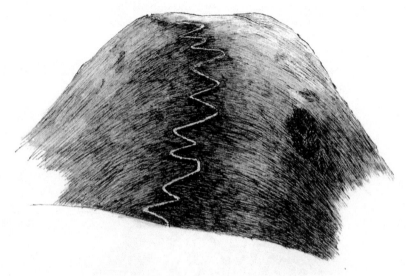

The weird yet magnificent path up Sail

Sail is an unremarkable rounded lump of a hill, and the climb up it was once a tedious slog that had become heavily eroded. The solution, as in many places, was to build a stone path. Sail's path, however, is uniquely weird: a long sine-wave snaking up the hill-side in nine oscillations from bottom to top[9]. Surely this was designed and built by a road engineer? Maybe a restless designer of motorways who needed something to do in the evenings and weekends? It is well engineered, with a broad, flat surface raised up on embankments one metre or more above the surrounding fellside, and just as a well-designed motorway is easy to drive on, so is this easy to walk on. You rapidly progress up the fell with remarkably little effort. The erosion has certainly been halted (the scars of the old path are just visible) and I suppose one should be grateful, but walking this path is an experience quite unlike fell walking anywhere else in the Lakes.

Sail's summit offers few reasons to linger – especially when the next stage of the walk is so good. After a short drop of a hundred feet or so the path proceeds along The Scar: a rough, rocky, windy ridge with steep drops on either side as it rises to the top of Crag Hill. This is one of those unsung short walks that help make the whole day worthwhile.

---

[9] In fact the path starts not at the bottom of Sail but on the descent from Scar Crags, adding another three waves, making twelve in all.

At first sight Crag Hill seems to be missing from Wainwright's guides, an omission that would be inexplicable given the hill's impressive bulk and its prominence on the OS map. It isn't missing of course, but the old boy preferred the name Eel Crag on the grounds of long use, while noting that it was 'unfortunate and inaccurate'. The OS reserves the name Eel Crag only for the fell's craggy northern end.

The summit is marked by an old trig point, but in 2014 it had been toppled, whether by the elements or deliberate act, I can't say.

The toppled trig point on Crag Hill. A rough cairn has been built beside it as an approximate substitute.

It is easy enough to explore the broad, flat, stony summit, but it's more rewarding to walk above the crags on the north-east face and peer down to Coledale and the Hause below, with the long ridge-line of Whiteside, Hopegill Head and Grisedale Pike stretching off into the distance. To the south there is a large tilted plane, like a giant's broken breakfast table; this is Wandhope Moss, a potential route down to Buttermere, which is just coming into sight.

The Buttermere fells seen from Crag Hill

Next in line is Grasmoor, whose summit is an even larger plateau of grass and stones that the wind rips across. It has a shelter at the top, cleverly divided into numerous cubby-holes so that it should be possible to find respite from the wind, if not the rain, whichever direction it's blowing. Sitting here eating lunch I watched several groups of people arriving and leaving pretty smartly, driven off by the weather, but they missed the best views in their haste. Dove Crag is well worth a detour to the north-east side (its position and shape echoes Eel Crag, passed earlier); it's possible to get a view of it from the northern tip of Grasmoor and from other viewpoints along the edge. And then there is the sight of Gasgale Crags over the valley to the north – an impressively long line of repeated gullies and scree runs.

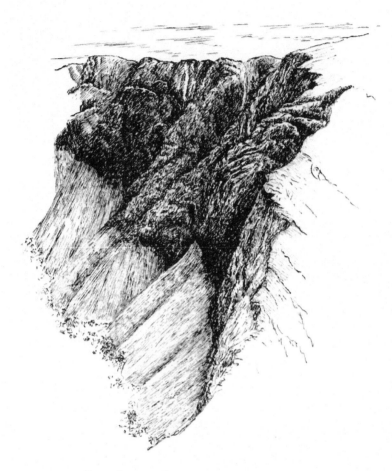

Dove Crag, on Grasmoor, seen from Gasgale Crag

Gasgale Crag seen from Dove Crag

Cat Bells and a long walk to Buttermere

The name refers to the wild cats that were common in the Lake District until the middle of the 19th century when the last one was killed. They were fierce, and regarded as a menace. It's hard to imagine them living on Cat Bells now, not only because of the almost total lack of cover, the fell having long been cleared of deep vegetation, but also because of the huge numbers of walkers, strollers, dawdlers, wanderers, dreamers and long-suffering stragglers who now visit it.

Its popularity is justified. It provides a genuine fell walk, with a tough ascent from the north end and a long, easy stroll along the ridge with outstanding views in all directions, yet it is short enough and easy enough for people of many degrees of fitness and ability to enjoy. It also lies on what is one of my favourite day-long walks, from Keswick to Buttermere.

Cat Bells through the rain: even in this weather it's worth a visit

There is a car park at the north end, but a great walk can be made even better by walking from Keswick, following the footpath over the meadows to Portinscale. In the fifteen minutes it takes there's time to admire Skiddaw, and the growing outlines of the great ridges to the left; a little surprisingly, the more distant Causey Pike ridge comes into view first. Beyond Portinscale the path ambles pleasantly through woods until, on reaching a clearing, there is a sudden and startling view of Cat Bells rising abruptly above a line of trees a few hundred yards ahead. There's something incongruous about the sight; there you are, in a flat field, with trees before and behind, and this huge, steeply sided ridge thrusting itself upwards, seemingly quite out of place and scale.

Cat Bells rising over the trees

Cat Bells must be one of the most popular walks in the Lakes; it certainly feels that way, as you join the crowds making their way up from the car park. It may only be a small fell (1,480 feet high) but it can still assert itself, and the climb is steep enough to leave many first-time fellwalkers gasping for breath. The path has been repaired and built up, but there are stretches where the rocky nature of the ridge defeats the path builders, and the route is marked by boot-polished rocks and trampled rubble. On one rocky prominence there is a plaque in memory of the British social reformer Thomas Arthur Leonard (1864–1948), who declared that 'The best things any mortal hath are those which every mortal shares' – a sentiment easily accepted while in this place, if too easily forgotten afterwards.

It would be hard to get lost once up on the ridge, except maybe in the worst mist. The summit offers an unsurpassed view of Skiddaw, with Blencathra beyond, and down below the beautiful Derwent Water, dotted with wooded islands. On the other side is Causey Pike, its bobbled, leaning summit clearly visible, while ahead lie the high fells that overlook Buttermere. There's a dip down to the bottom of Maiden Moor, after which the crowds thin out, some turning left to return along the lake-side, others right, to the Newlands Valley[10].

---

[10] On my last visit two people asked me 'how do I get back?' I was flattered they thought I looked like someone who might know, but dismayed that anyone could be up there and not know where they were.

Maiden Moor has an alluring name but it's not such an interesting fell to climb. The ascent crosses a broad flat area that looks from a distance like a tilted table top. From the top there is a more-or-less level walk of about two kilometres to the splendidly named High Spy, easily identified by the huge cairn at its summit. From here there are good views to the back of Dale Head and Hindscarth; Dale Head has its own Great Gable, a small set of crags at its foot, while the gullies running down the side of Hindscarth look like great wounds slashed into the fell.

Looking towards Maiden Moor, in the middle distance

Dalehead Tarn is a good place to rest. The source of Newlands Beck, it lies at the head of a rough little gully through which the beck churns and gurgles its way over the rocks. The steep walls of the gully frame an exciting view up the valley and along the flanks of Hindscarth.

Next is Dale Head. From the tarn, Dale Head presents itself as an obstacle rather than an objective – a steep, rounded fellside that promises little but toil. It has, of course, been damaged by boots, and in 2014 a new path was being built; the workers were still at the stage of digging into the fell and manoeuvring boulders into place before filling the joints with peat and rubble. The exposed boulders were huge, all carefully wedged in against each other, bonded in mutual support, so that the new path looked like it would last a thousand years or more. It was impossible not to be mightily impressed by the labour and craft that went into it. Yet there was a problem, because this new path goes straight up the slope, with barely a zig or a zag. Consequently it's hard work, each step from one boulder to the next requiring a serious expenditure of energy to haul yourself up. Descending steep paths like this is equally difficult, with large steps and a vertiginous dizziness induced by the steep drop before you.

> Why build a path in this way, with the risk that it will not be used as people seek easier routes on grass? I have two theories. One is that these paths are designed by the muscle-bound twenty-somethings who build them and who cannot see any problem or imagine what the experience is like for other walkers. The other is simple economics: building straight up and down is shorter and therefore cheaper.

Hindscarth Edge is one of the highlights of this walk. The edge runs for a kilometre, high above Honister Pass, directly opposite Fleetwith Pike's near-vertical crags. Even if by this stage in the day your legs are getting tired, it's worth delaying here to spend time simply gazing across the abyss. Huge spaces like this don't just look special, they sound special too, full of murmuring airy conversations that fill your ears while you peer into the vast empty cathedrals of earth and sky; small sounds rise from far below – a sheep bleating, a dog barking – while the breeze whispers over the grass at your feet, gently tugging at your hood or the cords of your rucksack. I have known confident, noisy men struck dumb by this experience.

It is as well to make the best of Hindscarth Edge because, after a sharp rocky descent, you're faced with the long, slow haul up Robinson, a great duffer of a fell with little to redeem it. It isn't particularly obvious where the top is, and after locating it you're faced with a long march across Buttermere Moss – a dreary slog over boot-sucking bog. Just as patience is running out there is a sudden redemption, because the final descent to Buttermere, off High Snockrigg, is unexpectedly glorious: steeply angled down the side of the fell on springy turf, with gurgling, rocky streams to cross and the sparkling waters of Crummock Water laid out before you.

Buttermere

One theory says the pretty name has nothing to do with butter but rather

Burthat, a fierce local warrior remembered for resisting the Normans. That's an attractive proposition, unless you think the name is really derived from *butere*, the old English word for dairy pastures. Well, the cows are still there in the pastures down by the lake, and while Burthat no doubt had many admirable qualities, the association with *butere* seems more probable in this lovely place.

The name applies to both the lake and the village, and I've always thought Buttermere to be one of Lakeland's most beautiful lakes, sitting in a compact glacial valley, walled on one side by dramatic mountains that plunge steeply down to the water's edge.

The village is tiny: two hotels, both with bars that welcome walkers (one of them associated with a tragic-romantic tale from two hundred years ago); a farm, a chapel, a youth hostel, a campsite, and little else in the way of buildings. The chapel has a memorial window dedicated to Wainwright that looks out over the lake to Haystacks, the fell about which he wrote so much and where his ashes are scattered.

From the village it's a short walk down to the shore where, sometimes, when the weather is good and it's too early in the morning for the wind to have disturbed the water's surface, Fleetwith Pike and its neighbouring fells can be seen perfectly reflected, upside down, in the depths.

Fleetwith Pike and Haystacks reflected in the waters of Buttermere

There is an easy walk around the lake's perimeter, taking about two hours at a leisurely pace and providing any visitor with an education in natural beauty. It even has a rock tunnel on the eastern shore, said to have been cut by the inmates of a workhouse on the slopes above.

One of the entrances to the lakeside rock tunnel, Buttermere

The west and southern sides of the lake are the most impressive, with the steep wooded slopes of High Stile and High Crag hanging high over the south-western shores, and Red Pike[11] just out of sight behind The Dodd. Beyond them, curving round the southern end of the lake, are Haystacks and Fleetwith Pike. This great arc of fells makes for a full day's walking, with the option of cutting it short at Scarth Gap, the pass that links Buttermere to the next valley, Ennerdale.

---

[11] That's a great name for a mountain. So great I fact that there is another Red Pike 5km south of here, overlooking the Mosedale valley. Buttermere's Red Pike is well named however, because it really is red, its soil stained with the red mineral syenite.

The wooded slopes leading up to The Dodd and High Stile

The ascent of Red Pike begins with a climb of sinew-cracking steepness through the woods at the lakeside. It's a built-up path, with well-set rocks, old enough now to look like it has always been there, the stones cushioned with green moss and ferns. From the top of the Pike there's a ridge route south-east over High Stile and High Crag towards Scarth Gap; it's easy to follow in clear weather, but can be confusing in mist, when a compass is essential.

From High Crag to Scarth Gap, much of the descent is over a sliding mass of loose rock, and consequently is hard work. Yet it turns out that there is a man-made rock path here, lost under the ever shifting and tumbling stones.

I once met two men up there armed with shovels and sturdy brooms, digging out the path. They had uncovered several hundred yards when we met, and were about to head down for lunch, which they did at speed, flexing taut sun-burnt leg muscles as they carried their shovels and brooms on their shoulders, leaving me far behind.

That was a few years ago; on a more recent visit I found that the path had been extended almost all the way down to Scarth Gap and, sadly, not in a good way. It's another precipitously steep path, going almost straight down the fellside with no twists or turns to break the gradient, making it tiring and dizzying. After trying to set a good example and stick with the path I realised I was falling far behind others who had given up and opted to use the grass and scree slopes on either side. I soon joined them. Looking back from the bottom, it was possible to see not only the 'improved' path, but also the ghostly mark of the old one, disused now, but clearly zig-zagging down the fellside like all well-designed paths should.

One of the many crags on High Crag

From Scarth Gap you can drop down to Buttermere, or cross over to Ennerdale, but most people eagerly carry on up the looming mound of rock directly in front: Haystacks. Made famous by Wainwright, who regarded it as one of his favourite fells, it's a small-scale rocky wonderland, full of scrambles, miniature tarns, hidden surprises and splendid views back over Buttermere, to Pillar, and round to Great Gable and the Sca Fells.

65

A view of Haystacks across Buttermere

One of the highpoints of this walk comes right after Haystacks. After passing Innominate Tarn, the path proceeds, with a precipitous drop on the left and the looming mass of Green Crag ahead, and at Black Beck a view over Buttermere suddenly appears, framed by the walls of a steep crevice.

Buttermere seen from Black Beck Tarn crags

After traversing the back of Green Crag it's possible to drop down to Warnscale Bottom via either of two paths that follow Warnscale (the mountain stream that tumbles down to the lake below): one above it, the other below. Neither is easy to find in the confusion of boulders and criss-crossing tracks; the upper path in particular starts after something of a dog's leg diversion above the stream, but is visible crossing the rising ground ahead.

If the paths are not obvious, Dubs Quarry certainly is. A mass of spoil heaps and broken-down buildings spread out over the face of the fell, it was part of the Honister Slate mines that have operated here since the early 18th century. Its heyday was in the late 19th century, but after that it fell into decline, eventually closing in 1989. Then, in 1997, it was reopened by an extraordinary man called Mark Weir, and became a successful producer of slate as well as a tourist attraction. Mr Weir was killed in a helicopter crash in 2011, but the mine is still open, producing slate and entertaining the tourists who visit it. You don't have to slog all the way there by foot over Haystacks to reach it: the entrance is on the roadside on Honister pass, with parking and a tea room where you are invited to pay whatever you think the tea is worth.

The path to Fleetwith Pike lies among the quarry roads and workings and may take some searching out. Keep going north-east, uphill, until you meet it; go too far and you'll face an eye-boggling drop down to Honister Pass, far below[12]. From the top of the Pike, in clear weather, there is a truly huge view encompassing Buttermere and Crummock, Pillar, Kirk Fell, Great Gable and the Sca Fells. The descent is delightful – a rocky scramble down the mountain's edge, always a little challenging and always with the mountain behind you and the lake spread out in front. From the shore of Buttermere you can see this path shining in the sunshine, polished by all the boots that have passed over it.

Crummock Water

Crummock isn't on the route to any of the giants, yet it is a lake of great beauty and will reward your interest in its own quiet way, especially on a long summer's evening, when a walk around its shores provides a quiet, perfect

---

[12] The active quarry workings may oblige you to change your route. There is another path that involves doubling back some way along a quarry road and then branching off to the right, up to the summit.

end to the day. From the pump house at its northern end the view is straight out of a Romantic landscape painting, full of classic grandeur, dramatic crags, wooded slopes, shining water and the ever-changing skies.

There is human history too: iron was once mined on the slopes of Mellbreak, the fell on the western shore, while Cinderdale Common on the opposite side gets its name from the smelting that used to take place there. The mine has gone, but brown streaks in Mellbreak's rocks betray the continued presence of iron.

Looking across Crummock Water towards the high fells

On the return to Buttermere, after passing beneath Mellbreak, it's possible to take a detour to the right for half a mile or so to visit Scale Force waterfall, hidden away in a deep cleft in the rock. To get the best view you have to climb a large rock step; Wainwright drew this with a ladder leaning up against it, but that is long gone and you now have to scramble up. It's easy enough – although you might get wet – and then you enter a green, damp, shadowed little world, filled with the noise of the water falling in an unbroken vertical drop of 170 feet down into a rock pool, the highest waterfall in the Lake District.

Scale Force

The whole area between Buttermere and Crummock is quite lovely and filled with character. From the Fish Hotel in the village it's possible to walk beside Mill Beck to the shore of Crummock Water, passing through deep meadows and woodland down to the shingle shore. Cattle stand quietly among the reeds in the water meadows, smoke slowly curls up from a camper's fire, a bird calls clearly over the lake, and it seems that this is a scene that has remained unchanged for centuries.

On summer evenings the setting sun sends shafts of light down over the lake, painting Fleetwith Pike a delicate pink for just a few moments until the shadows fall.

The tale of Mary Robinson

In 1792 Captain Joseph Budworth, a soldier who had lost an arm at the siege of Gibraltar, was on a tour of the Lake District gathering material for a small book he later published called *A Fortnight's Ramble to the Lakes in Westmoreland, Lancashire, and Cumberland*. Among the many things of beauty he saw and recorded, the one that made the greatest impression on him was the landlord's daughter at the Fish Inn, Buttermere. He wrote about Mary Robinson in his book, praising her beauty in passages of purple prose, thus drawing her to the attention of the curious and the hopeful, who flocked to the Inn to admire and woo her.

One of these was Colonel Alexander Augustus Hope, the brother of one Lord Hopetown. He arrived at the Inn, saw Mary, and after a whirlwind romance lasting three months, married her.

All of which came as a surprise to the real Colonel Alexander Augustus Hope, who was at that time in Vienna, where he was alerted by his father. There had of course been some suspicions; a man of distinction landing in a backwater like Buttermere and marrying well below himself was bound to attract attention and gossip. Coleridge in particular had had serious doubts, and had written to that effect in the local newspapers.

So, with the fraud exposed, the Colonel, now known under his real name of John Hatfield, fled. Arrest warrants were issued, and he was eventually captured in Wales. It turned out he was well known as a fraudster and had plenty of 'form' back in London; worse still, he was already married, with children. He was taken to Carlisle where he was tried, not on a charge of bigamy, but of fraudulently franking letters – evidently a much more serious matter: found guilty, he was, in the manner of the times, hanged.

Later, Budworth wrote that he regretted ever having drawn attention to Mary, who was only about fifteen years old when he first saw her and was pregnant when Hatfield was hanged. But four years later she married a local farmer with whom she had four children in what seems to have been a contented marriage. She died in 1837.

The story has been re-told many times. Coleridge and Wordsworth took a keen interest, attending the trial in Carlisle, and Melvyn Bragg wrote a fictionalised version of it in *The Maid of Buttermere*.

Ennerdale and an ascent of Pillar

Ennerdale is one of the Lake District's more remote valleys by virtue of its position on the western edge, leaving it somewhat isolated from the main flow of visitors, who generally arrive on the east. It's not a lonely valley however, because it features in Wainwright's Coast to Coast Walk – acronymically known as the C2C – and the hotels and B&Bs in Ennerdale Bridge and other villages at the valley's western end are kept busy with a procession of walkers, still full of optimism about their chances after only one day's walk from the starting point at St Bees.

Ennerdale is a walker's valley, not only because of the C2C path, but because cars are banned. The road to the southern shore ends at a car park where the River Ehen flows out of the lake; most of the C2C walkers pass by here, to follow the lake-shore path beneath Angler's Crag. To the north, the narrow road from Ennerdale Bridge meanders along through pretty lowland farming country, with the mountains in the background and the lake occasionally flashing blue through the trees, until it brings you to the car park beneath Bowness Knot, where there is a barrier across the road. From there it's a long haul on foot along the lakeside track, three miles to the foot of Pillar (if that's the main objective) and six miles added to the day's total walking. Much of that six miles is spent in or close to something else Ennerdale is famous for: its Forestry Commission plantations.

These plantations – the word is more fitting than 'forest' – date from the 1930s when the newly established Forestry Commission set about planting trees here, millions of them. They chose larch and spruce, trees they could grow quickly to provide timber with long straight trunks for buildings, fencing and telegraph poles. The new forests were controversial, partly because they were of non-native species, but mainly because of the ruthlessly industrial scale of the plantations, and the Commission's disregard for their appearance or their impact on wildlife and walkers. The trees were densely packed together, so that it was nigh impossible to pass between them, while the lack of sunlight and oppressive silence meant they were claustrophobic places, easy to get lost in and best avoided. Sure, there were tracks cut through them for the logging machinery, but they were no substitute for the older paths made by and for people, and in any case they were routed to suit the needs of loggers not walkers, offering little in the way of views other than of a monotonous dark wall of spruce trees to the left, the right and ahead.

In more recent times the Forestry Commission has tried to mend its ways and no longer sees the Lake District primarily as a timber production facility, although timber still is an important part of its remit. Consequently the plantations are changing. Many of them reached commercial maturity long ago and have been felled, leaving clearings that are being replanted with a broader mix of trees. Disease is also taking its toll; in 2014 the larch trees were dying off in large numbers, infected by Phytophthora ramorum, first identified in this country in 2009. But there is a more positive source of change too: a rewilding project being carried out by a partnership between the Forestry Commission, the National Trust, Natural England and United Utilities. This has the declared aim of enabling *'the evolution of Ennerdale as a wild valley for the benefit of people, relying more on natural processes to shape its landscape and ecology'*[13]. In other words, to let nature get on with it. This is a project to be watched with interest, not only because there is intrinsic value in creating a genuine wilderness, but also to help answer the question of what happens when the sheep leave?

The task for today, however, is to tackle Pillar. The walk from Bowness car park follows a wide track along the lake shore. Pillar dominates the view ahead, trees permitting, with the unmistakeable outline of Pillar Rock protruding from it, like a gigantic single tooth standing out from a lower jaw.

Pillar seen over Ennerdale Water

Beyond the lake the track passes an outdoor field centre and the Youth Hostel, with the River Liza down below. Eventually – and maybe with some relief – you arrive at the Memorial Bridge, situated a little way from the road, down a slope. Pillar is now directly in front of you, on the other side of the river, its dark mass looming precipitously above and looking a little intimidating, as all proper mountains should.

---

[13] Quoted from the Wild Ennerdale website, www.wildennerdale.co.uk

After crossing the little wooden bridge you join a forestry path to the right for a few yards until a small cairn, easily missed, marks the start of the ascent. First impressions are that this path is hardly used at all, for it is little more than a light, intermittent scuffing of the surface (although this does change further up). Wainwright described the lower section of this ascent as a slog through forestry plantations that he hated, but now the trees have been cleared, leaving a dwarf forest of moss-covered stumps, and in good weather if the path is temporarily lost the way ahead is obvious enough: keep the stream to your left and Pillar Rock directly above. Mostly the way is steep but easy, with only one place where there's a rough scramble over loose rocks above the stream, easily skirted by moving to the right.

Pillar Rock seen from below on the path from the Memorial Bridge

Eventually the ground levels off in Pillar Cove, a depression at the foot of the Rock. Pillar Rock scarcely needs a 'Climbers Only' notice, for it is dark and forbiddingly threatening, with a narrow gully cut into it and a scattering of tumbled rocks at its base. In gusty weather the wind howls; in the calm there is an ominous echo. Fortunately the Rock does not mark the end of the way: the path leads to the left, through the Cove, over some hefty boulders and up to Robinson's Cairn – a large monument that is visible on the skyline long before you reach it.

Pillar Rock and Robinson's Cairn. Robinson was a local man from Lorton, and the cairn was raised by his friends – one hundred of them according to the cairn's plaque – after he died in 1907

At this point there is a choice between two routes, both of them excellent. One is to double back from the cairn towards Pillar Rock and follow the Shamrock Traverse up above Pisgah and then up the loose rocky slope to the top of Pillar. If that sounds straightforward, it's not: describing the walk in such a compact sentence hardly does it any justice at all. In the first place, Shamrock Traverse runs up a slope above the rockface called, unsurprisingly, Shamrock. The name is nothing to do with botany but sham-rock, meaning not the real Pillar Rock; this not-the-real-rock is a vertical drop, and the traverse rises across it at an angle, but with sections of its walking surface sloping down towards the drop. That would not be so bad, but as with many paths the difficulty lies in the erosion it has suffered, leaving it a tricky mix of polished and broken rocks. Once this has been passed there is a terrific rear-view of Pillar Rock itself with, very likely, some climbers dangling off it. There are two heights visible: Pisgah is the nearest, and High Man beyond it. The two are separated by the Jordon (those early climbers really liked their Old Testament names). The gap between the traverse and Pisgah is frustratingly narrow, but this is where walking ends and climbing begins, so Pisgah is not an option. No, our route is up the slope behind, which is troublesome because of its steepness and the looseness of the scree underfoot. The surest way to tackle it is to take a deep breath and a metaphorical run and keep going doggedly, not looking back until the gradient levels off towards the top.

The alternative from Robinson's Cairn is to go along the high-level route – a climbers' traverse that passes high up, more or less at a level gradient, below the crags and gullies of Pillar, until it pops up just above the head of Black Sail Pass. In clear weather this is a magnificent walk, with a steep drop to one side, the crags towering above on the other, and with great views of the valley below and of Great Gable ahead. The going is safe but challenging enough to speed one's heart rate quite satisfyingly. It is most frequently walked in the opposite direction, from Black Sail towards Robinson's Cairn, as an alternative route up Pillar, but it's equally good either way round.

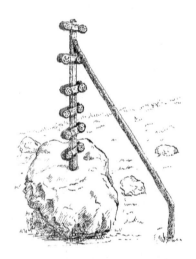

An old fence post on Pillar. It still has its tensioning mechanisms, rusted solid.

Once the ridge above Black Sail Pass is reached the way up Pillar is obvious enough; not hugely interesting in itself but with excellent views all round, particularly back towards Great Gable and over to the Sca Fell range.

The summit is maybe a disappointment after the earlier challenges of the ascent, being relatively smooth and domed, but among the various shelters scattered about there is one designed like a giant rock armchair in which you can sit and contemplate the Buttermere ranges opposite. There is also a good view of Pillar Rock from above, if you stand close to the north-east edge of the dome.

Great Gable seen from Pillar

Scafell Pike and Sca Fell, seen from Pillar

The most direct route back to Ennerdale is to take a bee-line north-west over White Pike, but it's easy to be seduced by the cairned and rocky path leading south-west, down to Wind Gap. It begins innocuously enough, rolling off the dome and getting progressively steeper, but like all seducers it draws you on and on until you find you've gone too far and can't turn back.

Or, more prosaically, tired legs insist that having descended that far you may as well continue all the way down to the gap, where a path drops off to the right down into the broad and empty Windgap Cove. This way seems to be little used and the path fades out and back again as you lose height, while behind the arc of fells from Pillar to Scoat to Steeple is impressive. Cattle graze on the lower slopes of White Pike, and eventually the line of plantations is reached again.

The Ordnance Survey map indicates a route that traces the northern boundary of the plantation for a short distance, crosses a beck, and then enters the woods, with a clear route all the way down to the River Liza at the valley's bottom. In practice this did not quite work out for me. The bridge over the beck was no more than a piece of old fencing thrown across the water, bouncing and wobbling as I crossed it. The path into the trees was clear at first, but the ground underfoot was very boggy and the trees pressed closer and closer together until, without warning, my leg sank knee-deep into bog and, after hauling myself out, I found that the path had completely disappeared. Instead the ground was now a soggy mess of bog and tangled roots, while the trees were so close together that I had to force my way through them, holding my map-case up in front of my face with both hands to protect it from the sharp pine needles. Progress was slow, exasperating and unpleasant. This was indeed a classic Forestry Commission plantation: dark, disorienting, and so densely planted as to be virtually impassable.

The 'bridge' on High Beck, just before entering the forestry plantations

This experience did little to endear me to the Forestry Commission's methods, but at the bottom of the slope, having found the valley path, progress was much more enjoyable, through mixed woodland with the River Liza once again at my side. By the time I reached the lake, and crossed over to the path on its north side, evening was setting in and a calm had settled over the valley, the setting sun sending its beams the full length of the lake to the mountains beyond, lighting them orange and gold.

That evening the concerned landlady at the B&B where I was staying asked what had happened to my forearms; they were covered in scratches and streaked with blood. I hadn't even noticed.

5   THE NORTH: SKIDDAW AND BLENCATHRA

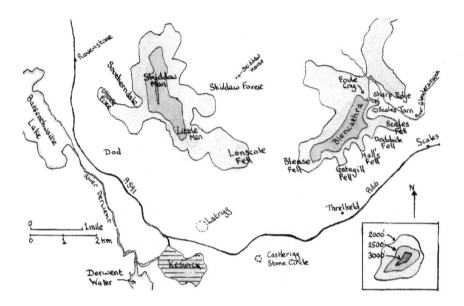

Skiddaw

Poor old Skiddaw. After all, it has so much going for it. It has a perfect name for a mountain, ancient and resonant, those five consonants lending it a hard, rocky feel, just like the real thing. It has a glorious position, sitting at the north end of the Lakes above Keswick and Derwent Water, isolated from all the other mountains, its almost perfectly symmetrical profile recognisable from miles away as if it were a giant figure crouched down to look benignly over the lake, its arms spread out protectively on either side. Its mood and colours change from season to season, sometimes purple and green, sometimes grey, sometimes capped with snow, sometimes dappled with sunlight and the shadows of passing clouds. On bad days it sulks while the rain slants down, shrouded in heavy grey clouds that roll down to its lowest slopes.

No, Skiddaw certainly offers lots of promise. The problem with Skiddaw is that when you get really close up with your boots on, it is, to be honest, just a tiny bit dull.

It's partly a question of attitude. If Skiddaw were in, say, Yorkshire, its praises would be widely sung as the greatest mountain in the county and thus all of England. If it has an element of dullness it's only relative to its rougher, craggier neighbours to the south – show-offs like Sca Fell and Bow Fell. Skiddaw does not offer crags or dramatic waterfalls, it has no scree or alarming gullies. What is has, in the experience of the many people who toil up from the car park at Latrigg, is a long grind of an ascent up a smooth slope on a clear, broad, unvarying path, with little more to be seen in front than the next false summit. It may be dull, but it's not an easy climb; after all, starting from Keswick, which is perfectly feasible, you would be faced with an ascent of 850 metres (about 2,800 feet) – more than enough to test lungs and leg muscles – while the weather up there can be as brutal as anywhere else in the Lakes. It's just that you'll be walking up a path of monotony. Wainwright wrote that people had once driven cars up here, and while that sounds a little fanciful now, it tells you something of what to expect.

However, Skiddaw is also a bit special. It doesn't just sound ancient by name; its rocks, known as Skiddaw Slate, are the oldest in the Lakes, as much as 500 million years old, laid down in seas so long ago it's almost unimaginable to us now. They were there long before the volcanic masses of Sca Fell and its colleagues in the central area appeared, and its rounded contours speak of the vast periods of time over which it has been battered and shaped by the weather and geological forces. It's worth pondering that while trudging up its slopes, wondering if you could have spent your time better on something more dramatic. The old guardian of the north doesn't have to apologise for dullness or anything else, for he pre-dates everything around him, having watched over the surrounding lakes and mountains as they were born.

And anyway, an ascent of Skiddaw does not have to be dull. It only has this reputation because so many people have walked up from Latrigg Fell, but there are much better routes, and one of them is via Ullock Pike.

The walk starts near the Ravenstone Hotel, north-west of Keswick on the A591. There is a bus that stops there, although it's a very infrequent service. The path plunges into woodland up a very steep slope that continues up and above the tree-line, and a long ridge that rises towards Ullock Pike. From this point onwards the great thing about this path is the huge view that it supplies in every direction. Behind you, to the north, you can see further and further as you rise, over the Solway Firth and beyond into Scotland. There are wind turbines scattered across those plains and you can see them lined up in rows out across the waters of the Firth, their blades swishing round in a calm, rhythmic, elegant motion as they suck up energy from the air around them. Below, on the right, lie the calm, broad waters of Bassenthwaite Lake, with the North West fells beyond. In front lies the ridge path, turning and twisting, while on the left there is a huge rounded and bleak-looking valley, Southerndale, with your walk's highest point beyond it. The head of this valley, at Carl Side, is the link between the ridge and Skiddaw, and eventually the path can be seen in the distance, slanting up the grey flanks of the mountain.

There are a couple of places where light scrambling is called for, but soon Ullock Pike is reached. This is a great lookout point; somewhere to stop for a drink while you gaze out over the Bassenthwaite valley to the North West fells, which seem so numerous, their hump-backed profiles, like a school of whales, fading away into the hazy distance, while a little further to the left is Keswick and Derwent Water. In good weather the Sca Fell range might be visible on the horizon, probably shrouded in cloud, a little sinister-looking even on a clear day.

The path continues to Carl Side where it veers off to the left, crossing the end of Southerndale and up the side of Skiddaw. This flank of the mountain is covered with broken stone fragments, grey pieces of Skiddaw Slate that have been broken apart by the weather and scattered over the fellside like industrial waste. Skiddaw may be made of slate, but it is slate that crumbles easily and it cannot be used successfully for building. However, it is not entirely without use; it's impossible not to notice how the stones chink together musically as you walk on them, and people have made tuned percussion instruments from them, called lithophones; Ruskin had one at his home in Brantwood which can still be seen by visitors today (admittedly, it was made with Coniston slate).

At the top of the slope you are, more or less, at the summit. Skiddaw's roof is a long, broad, rolling plain and the true summit is not immediately obvious, but there is a trig point and, nearby, a stone shelter. Walk beyond it, to the north, for more great views of the Solway Firth and Scotland.

There are no obstacles to block the view on Skiddaw; no rocks, no walls, no trees. The rolling and comparatively drab moorland to the east is called Skiddaw Forest, yet it doesn't have a single tree in it – apart from a tiny plantation around Skiddaw House, once a shooting lodge and now a YHA bunkhouse.

Because of the landscape's emptiness the path ahead, to the south, is clear. The main path curves off grandly to the left, unexpectedly avoiding the lesser summit of Little Man, while another, not marked on the OS map but a serious, well-used path nevertheless, follows the fence line up over Little Man. Having come this far it seems perverse to omit the little fella, unless the weather is bad. At the top there is a cairn built of a mix of stone and rusting old iron fence posts.

Looking back over Skiddaw Little Man with Ullock Pike in the distance

From there the way drops back down to the main path, which now proceeds in a broad curve, rather like a drive through a royal park, all the way down. I think claims of a car being driven up here are an exaggeration, although a large 4x4 might do it, or a tank. It's quite steep – particularly the last half mile or so – but the great thing now is that laid out before you are wonderful views over Derwent Water to Borrowdale and, a little further to the east, Helvellyn and its neighbours. I was last there in the spring, and the air was filled with the sound of skylarks high above, nigh impossible to locate against the blue sky, their songs tumbling out in a torrent of notes, ending abruptly as they suddenly plunged down to earth, only to be replaced immediately by a rival rising up out of the heather.

At the bottom you come to a road and a car park, but it's not far beyond that to the famous viewpoint on the top of Latrigg. From here you can look back to Skiddaw, where you've just been. When I was there, as the sun dropped, the fell's colours and rounded curves and the shadowed valley below Little Man were all dramatically prominent, and it occurred to me that maybe Skiddaw is just one of those mountains that is best enjoyed from a distance, rather than close up.

With that thought in mind, there is a pleasant walk off Latrigg through woodlands down into Keswick for a well-earned pint of beer and a good dinner.

The view of Skiddaw from Latrigg

The view over Derwent Water from Latrigg

Blencathra

As you approach the northern lakes via the main road from Penrith, Blencathra looms up directly in front: huge, rugged and even a little intimidating. For a while the road seems set on a collision course, before it veers off to the left, skirting around the base of the mountain, its buttresses and deep canyons hanging high overhead.

It's equally impressive when seen from the approach from Thirlmere, its flanks, ridges and canyons fanned out before you as if it was enacting a display to attract attention.

Blencathra actually has two names. Its alternative and possibly older name is Saddleback, and the saddle can indeed be seen from the eastern approach, a curving depression in the mountain's profile between the mini-peaks of Halls Fell Top and Foule Crag.

The fell shares some characteristics with its near-neighbour, Skiddaw. They are both made of Skiddaw Slate; they are both free-standing, offering no ridge walks to other fell-tops; and they both have rather uninteresting northern faces. However, where Blencathra is far superior to Skiddaw, and many other fells, is the brutal, rugged mountain scenery it displays on its southern side.

Viewed from the south, Blencathra is a long curving dome whose nearside has been gouged out with a series of deep gullies separated by giant buttresses. There are four of these gullies and five buttresses. Two of the five are wrap-around smooth fells, one at each end, but the middle three are imposing edifices, fanning out in great triangles from their narrow tops to their wide bases above the road. Then all along the top is a line of rocky crags that look completely impassable, except, perhaps, to climbers.

Blencathra seen from the south, over Thirlmere

From left to right the buttresses are: Blease Fell, Gategill Fell, Hall's Fell, Doddick Fell and Scales Fell; the gullies are known by the Gills flowing down them: Blease Gill, Gate Gill, Doddick Gill and Scaley Beck.

Each of the south-facing buttresses and gullies offers at least one route up, and they are all of varying degrees of ruggedness and difficulty. Here is one that is somewhere in the middle of the range; not too easy (no true mountain route should be) but well within the capabilities of most walkers.

It starts from Scales, where there is a small car park (not the one reserved for local residents but another, higher up in the trees) and a pub that is worth making a note of for the return. Walk a couple of hundred yards back down the main road towards Keswick, and then take the clearly signposted and trampled path, turning left once you're above the buildings. In a few minutes you reach Scaley Beck, where you will encounter what could be the toughest challenge you'll face all day. Crossing the beck is easy enough, but then you have to grapple with a small but particularly argumentative rock face, quite determined in its attempts to block your way. It comes as a real surprise, so early in the day.

After that the ascent of one of those buttresses, Doddick Fell, begins. Wainwright described a route that rises directly up the steep slope, and while a zigzag of steps can be made out and followed, it looks like many people now opt for an alternative that skirts the foot of the fell and rises up from the other side. Whichever you choose, it isn't long before you get to the backbone of the slope. From here on there's an imposing view of the summit high above and the craggy edge that curves round from Doddick to Hall's Fell, while on either side lie two of Blencathra's deep and stony gullies: Doddick Gill to the left and Scaley Beck to the right. There is no danger, just some huff and puff, while on pausing for breath and water one can turn around and enjoy the view that opens up southwards over the Vale of St John's to Helvellyn.

At the top of Doddick Fell you meet the much broader path that crosses over from Scales Fell, while directly in front is a drop down to Scales Tarn, almost perfectly circular and cupped by sheer-faced crags. There is a path, clear enough but not shown on the OS map, that leads down to the tarn, but for now let's keep to the summit, and the walk west, along the top of Blencathra's craggy southern face.

This is a surprisingly easy walk, although it can be very windy. The wide path follows the edge for about two kilometres over a series of little summits, perhaps the most impressive being above Hall's Fell, from where there's a challenging escape route down a path that twists and turns along the ridge. Moving west along Blencathra's extended summit, the contrast between the landscape on the left- and right-hand sides is striking. To the left, on the south, there is a steep drop over the cliffs, with the buttresses and their shadowy gullies falling away in a dizzying, rhythmic progression; to the right, on the north, there is rolling grass and heather stretching off for miles, with almost nothing calling out for exploration. Three miles away lies the back of Skiddaw, again with little to attract attention unless you have a special feeling for lonely, empty and slightly depressing countryside.

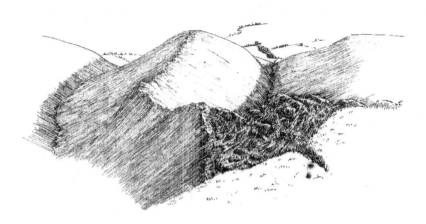

Looking down Hall's Fell

The buttresses are sufficiently exciting and exhilarating in themselves to warrant an expedition to Blencathra, but this mountain has something else – an even more famous sight and challenge up on the precipitous crags that form the backdrop to Scales Tarn: Sharp Edge.

Sharp Edge viewed from the slopes above Scales Tarn

Sharp Edge really is sharp; in fact it is sometimes called Razor Edge, although this name seems to have fallen out of use lately. I climbed it, once, many years ago, and that was enough. My recollection is that even though it is less well known than Striding Edge, which has a much more active publicity department, Sharp Edge is by far the more difficult climb. The reasons are simple: the stretch that gives it its name is very sharp indeed, and you are completely exposed, with precipitous drops on either side; it is made of slate that quickly becomes slippery when wet; there is a 'bad step' that requires an awkward manoeuvre and confidence in the grip of your boots; and the rocks are polished smooth by the passage of thousands of previous walkers.

So these days I'm content to watch other people climb Sharp Edge – or, in a few cases, descend it – while I sit on Foule Crag above, munching sandwiches and offering a few words of congratulation to the tense-faced people who make it to the top, some of them verging on hysterical cheeriness, others silent and avoiding eye-contact.

Sharp Edge seen from above

Sharp Edge is said to be classed as a Grade One Scramble, which means hands and feet are required, but no specialist equipment. You have to decide for yourself whether to attempt it: the accident statistics are available on the Web to help you.

There are good paths back to the pub, either over Scales Fell, or, from the tarn, beside Scales Beck. The beck flows into the Scottish-sounding River Glenderamackin, whose banks below Scales Fell are a long series of folds which are especially striking when low sunlight catches their crests.

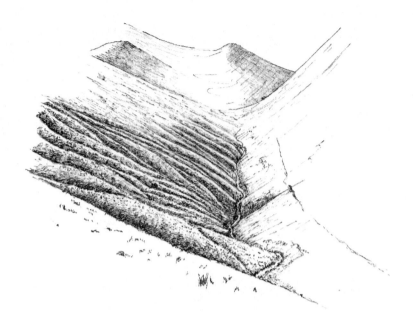

The folds in the slopes above the River Glenderamackin

Castlerigg Stone Circle

Blencathra forms a fitting backdrop to the enigmatic Castlerigg Stone Circle. This ring of standing stones, just outside Keswick, is thought to have been built as long ago as 3,000 BC. It would have taken considerable effort to build, yet its original purpose is long forgotten. Now, it is popular with tourists, photographers, artists and druids.

6   THE EAST

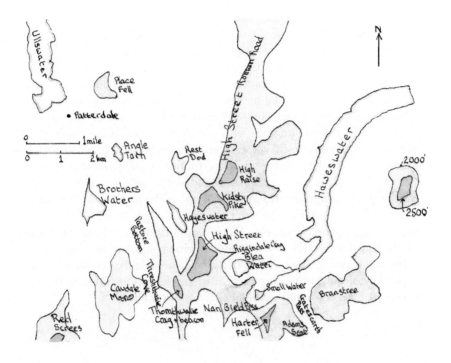

Patterdale

Patterdale Youth Hostel is unusual in that it was purpose-built in what must once have seemed a bold and modern style. Vaguely Scandinavian, the main building has steeply sloped roofs supported by great timber beams, while some of the outer buildings, where the dormitories are, have flat roofs with gardens on them. Now it looks a bit tired, the roof-gardens grow little more than weeds and the paintwork is well past its best. This is the way with so many youth hostels; the YHA does not seem to have the funds needed to maintain its buildings properly, and many are in a state of slow decline.

One source of business for Patterdale hostel is the village's position as a stopover point on the C2C, the coast-to-coast footpath from St Bees to Robin Hood's Bay. The hostel is used by many long-distance walkers, at this stage three days into their trip and mostly still optimistic about their chances, though perhaps edged with a little more realism than when we last met them at Ennerdale. The C2C is famous internationally, and many of the walkers are foreign: the Dutch were well represented when I was last in Patterdale YHA. I shared a dorm with three men, all doing the C2C. Two were travelling together, while the third had tagged along on the way. One of the pair, a Geordie, looked like he might be an ex-soldier: muscular, with cropped hair, and very organised. He was up and ready to go at 8am while his fellow traveller was still blundering about looking for his wash-bag, his clothes scattered all over the floor. The third was Dutch, with great ambitions for the walk but carrying one of the biggest rucksacks I've ever seen, loaded down with items that must all have seemed indispensable when he was in the hiking gear shop, credit card in hand. The three of them set off before me but I soon caught up with them, first with the Dutchman who was slowly toiling up the path, each step a hesitant and painful struggle, and then with the others who were waiting for him. The soldier was cheerful but clearly frustrated. Later I saw that he and his companion had abandoned their fellow traveller who was by then trailing far behind. That stage of the C2C, from Patterdale to Shap, is a tough 15 miles over the top of High Street and through much rough country with few – if any – opportunities to break the route on the way. Later in the day I wondered what became of the Dutchman; at the rate he was going there was no chance he would reach Shap before dark, if ever, but his weighty pack must surely have held everything he needed for a comfortable overnight stay out in the wild.

This fine fellow was all alone in a field in Patterdale

High Street

High Street is the name of both a mountain and an ancient roadway built by the Romans to move troops between Galava fort at Ambleside and Brougham fort just south of Penrith. Following a high contour, it may have been bleak but it was safer for troops marching in hostile country than the modern route over Kirkstone Pass and along Ullswater's shores, where ambush was a constant threat.

Starting from Patterdale the path up to High Street grinds its way diagonally up the slopes of the eastern fells overlooking the valley, with views to Helvellyn and over Brothers Water towards Kirkstone Pass. Once the first levels are reached the path winds around some hillocks and bumps before passing along the shore of Angle Tarn – a strangely shaped little tarn, quite dramatic despite its small size, with two small islands and, on the opposite shore, a line of miniature crags that give it the appearance of a scaled-down model of a full-size lake surrounded by towering fells. A little beyond that, Hayeswater comes into view (not to be confused with its near-homophonic neighbour, Haweswater, which is many times larger and two miles away). Hayeswater sits in a steeply sided glacial valley with a necklace of moraine hillocks all around its shores. Indeed, the surrounding slopes are so steep that the lake is more or less inaccessible except from its northern end, where there is a bridge and an old dam, for Hayeswater is a reservoir. Or at least it was: at the time of writing, after supplying water to the Ullswater communities for a century, there are plans to decommission the reservoir and return the lake to its natural state.

Angle Tarn: it looks grand, but is in fact a miniature landscape

Red deer live up here, but you have to stay alert to see them. They appear on the skyline in small groups of half a dozen or so, standing stock-still, carefully watching you; they saw you long before you saw them. After a few moments' contemplation they invariably bound away out of sight over the horizon.

The eastern slopes of Hayeswater are the flanks of High Street the mountain. The ascent is not so hard, because the path follows gentler contours east of the lake, rising up to the Straits of Riggindale, where a completely new view opens up straight down another glacial valley lying exactly at right-angles to Hayeswater's, with Kidsty Pike on its northern side, Riggindale Crag on its south, and Haweswater reservoir at its end.

The reservoir, built to supply water to Manchester, was completed in 1935 when the valley was flooded, submerging the villages of Mardale Green and Measand. When the water levels drop the ruined buildings emerge once again, only to sink back as the levels recover. From up on the Straits of Riggindale, Haweswater is some way off, but it is still possible to see the tell-tale tidemark along the water's edge – a sure sign of a man-made reservoir.

Looking down Riggindale Crag to Haweswater, in the distance.
Blea Tarn is on the right.

High Street the roadway extends north and south from here. To the north it follows lower rolling hills through a wild and somewhat bleak countryside, quite unlike the central fells of the Lake District, which it leaves behind. In the other direction it heads due south over the broad flat ridge of High Street, the fell-top. In clear weather there is a view of nearly all the rest of the Lake District fells from here: Coniston Old Man, Bowfell, the Sca Fells and Great Gable, the Helvellyn range, and Skiddaw and Blencathra away to the north.

On cloudy days you will have to be more forbearing, because the top of High Street is more than a tiny bit dull. Apart from the trig point, a long broken wall and a surfeit of bog, there is really very little at all: the grandeur is all at a distance. However, the place has a history, and with a little imagination there is no reason to be bored.

The area near the trig point is called Racecourse Hill on the OS maps because, however improbable it seems, that is what it was once used for during summer fairs that were held up here in the 18th and 19th centuries. Over to the west side of the crest there's a stone pathway, all of twenty feet wide and firm underfoot, that is presumably the course of the old Roman road; that road is ancient, and it's thought to have been in use long before the Romans engineered it for use by an occupying army. High Street may have a lonely and bleak aspect to it now, but it has been the site of much human activity over many centuries, and as you tramp across it with the wind and cold rain beating into your face you can reflect on how your experience is one that has been endured by many other people over millennia.

The trig point on High Street

Keeping south, it's hard to avoid heading towards a large pillar in the distance, a bold and obvious landmark that calls out 'this way please'. This is Thornthwaite Beacon: a stone column standing at the end of a long wall at the highest point of Thornthwaite Crag. Wainwright wrote that the column stood 14 feet high. Maybe it did in his time, but it looks a little shorter these days; indeed it isn't truly vertical and from some angles it looks like it has been buffeted out of alignment by many years of howling winds. Perhaps it has been. Anyway, it remains impressive and, like many of these large monuments, leaves you wondering who decided to build it and why, and, for that matter, how, for its height implies there must have been a platform to work from; it was not the work of one person on an idle Sunday afternoon.

Thornthwaite Beacon

In the short walk over to the beacon you will have passed the southern end of Hayeswater's valley, and now, to the west, there is another deep valley, lying parallel to the first and almost identical to it except for the absence of a lake. This will be our way back. From the beacon there is a moderately rough decent down to Threshthwaite Mouth, which is simultaneously the head of this new valley and of yet another one, much larger, running directly south down to Troutbeck and, eventually, to Windermere.

Looking north from Threshthwaite Mouth

Sitting on a rock looking north down the valley path yet to be taken, I watched two ravens high above in the sky. They wheeled about each other as they climbed higher and higher, then broke away to come tumbling down through the air, over and over, pulling out of the fall at the last moment only to start all over again, their croaking calls echoing across the valley. Maybe there was some utilitarian purpose to their actions – a blind response to the exigencies of life in a harsh landscape evolved over many thousands of years. Or maybe they were just playing and showing off, enjoying the experience of being alive and possessed of such aerobatic skills, their croaking a simple expression of joy. Watching them, I was pleased to imagine it was the latter.

The path down into the valley, which is nameless on the OS map (other than for Pasture Bottom at, well, the bottom), is eroded at the start but quite well built-up further down, easy enough but interminably long. As you descend, the sheer scale of the valley becomes clear; it's almost a physical sensation, the feeling of being small in a vast space. A tired but idle mind starts to wonder: was this valley really carved out by ice? Look at its volume: just how much ice was there? What became of the vast quantities of rock and earth that were stripped out? How long did it all take?

Later that day, after a pause to sketch Brothers Water, I walked back to Patterdale along the footpath that runs under the shadow of the eastern fells from the tiny hamlet of Hartsop. Wooded, with crags and fields and walls and views across to Helvellyn, the sun shining through at last and transforming the world from hard, cold grey to warm and golden, it was hard not to feel this was, in fact, the best part of the day's walk. It was the feeling of satisfaction at what had been done, the warmth of the evening sunshine, the beauty of that gentle walk – and the imminent prospect of a good dinner.

Looking over Brothers Water towards Kirkstone Pass. Drawn on the spot.

The far east

Haweswater is surprisingly remote, given that it's only a relatively short distance as the crow flies from the M6 and the A6. From the south, the drive from Shap follows ever-narrowing, winding country roads some way north of the lake to Bampton, before turning back south-west to follow the lakeside past the rather grand-looking Haweswater Hotel, built when the reservoir was constructed, right down to the car park at the southern end of the water.

Shap Abbey is at the end of a long single-track lane off the road to Bampton, set in a hollow beside the River Lowther. This massive tower still stands, and the outlines of many of the buildings of the abbey complex are visible. It is sobering to reflect on the scale of the original buildings, hidden away in such a remote place, long since reduced to ruins.

Gatescarth Pass rises up from the car park in a southerly direction. It twists and turns, but is surprisingly broad and well surfaced, with no severe gradients, and it provides a quick and easy ascent to the ridge leading on to Harter Fell[14]. It has the feel of a rough country road, and you half expect to see vehicles up there. Indeed I did, of a sort: there were shepherds working to round up their sheep, rolling along the road and across the fells in their squat fat-tyred vehicles, whistling and shouting commands to their sheepdogs who hurtled back and forth and up and down, clearly enjoying the whole

---

[14] Yet another name used more than once. There is another Harter Fell in the west, near Hardknott.

performance.

There's more to Gatescarth Pass than it being a quick way up the fells for quad-biking shepherds, for on one day a month it's open to vehicles as a leisure route, when 4x4s, motorbikes, quad bikes and others can go up there, provided they have a permit. There's time to grind up the road, take lots of photographs of the 4x4 from a low angle on a rough sharp bend, preferably with at least one wheel jutting out off the ground and the driver hanging one arm out of the window, post them on the internet and zoom off back down to the pub for lunch.

Meanwhile the walkers slog on. Before long the path levels off and swings round to the right, but on the skyline to the left a strange-looking monument stands all alone on the top of a modest rise called Adam's Seat. Leaving the main path to investigate, as you approach it looks more and more like a gravestone with a little mound of stones at its base. This rather mournful-looking edifice turns out to be an old boundary stone marking the borderline between Longsleddale and Shap, yet you wouldn't know it by examining the letters engraved on it: a large H on the south side and L on the north, each letter six inches high. They stand for the names of the land-owners of the time, H for Harrison, L for Lowther.

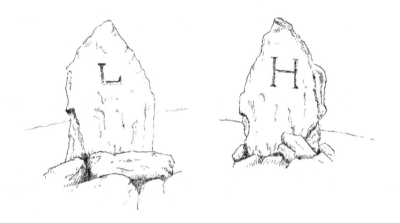

The two sides of the boundary stone on the top of Adam Seat

Harter Fell is the next objective. The path follows an easy rising course with increasingly long views of Haweswater opening up as height is gained. One of the very few occasions when Wainwright drew himself, or indeed anyone, in his Guides was in Book Two, *The Far Eastern Fells*, when he drew a view of Haweswater from up here, with him sitting with his back against a small cairn looking into the distance. The cairn has gone – it was in reality only a very small heap of stones on top of a larger rock, which is still there – and so, of course has Wainwright, leaving a Wainwright-shaped hole in a view that is otherwise almost unchanged since he drew it, sixty years ago.

The view over Hamesmater with a Wainwright-shaped hole

There are two cairns up here, both of them mounds of stone speared through with the twisted remains of iron fencing stabbing out in all directions. The second is the largest and most impressive, marking the summit and a popular place for people to stop and have lunch. With luck you might see the solitary Golden Eagle that lives somewhere in the Riggindale valley – a single male that has been seen sky-dancing in a forlorn attempt to attract a mate. Or perhaps not; I fell into conversation there with a loquacious

Geordie who said the bird had gone, but he did not know where. Maybe, after ten years of living here all alone, it had headed off to Scotland where its chances of finding a mate would be much better.

Looking north from Harter Fell, with Small Water down below, High Street and Riggindale in the distance

The drop down to Nan Bield Pass is not visible from the cairn on Harter Fell, but the path leading to it is, heading west before dipping over the edge of the fell, at which point the way becomes obvious and the view quite exciting, with a rough descent down to the arête separating Mardale from the Kentmere valley, with Mardale Ill Bell hanging above, the long line of Riggindale Crags in the distance, and a little of Blea Water just visible.

There is a crossing of paths at the bottom, with a large stone shelter, built like a giant's TV sofa, with a seat and high wings to keep the wind off; here you can sit and admire the view down into Mardale and over Haweswater.

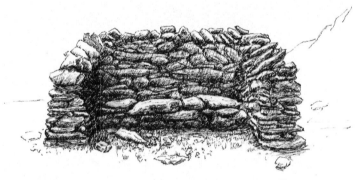

The bizarre stone sofa at the top of Nan Bield Pass. It's located on a medieval packhorse route between Kendal and Penrith, and the name, Nan Bield, is thought to mean 'Anne's shelter': Anne must have walked here long ago, and her sofa-shelter may be very old indeed.

Nan Bield pass is still busy today, not with packhorses but walkers, and, to my surprise at least, cyclists.

The rough but enjoyable descent down to the tarn, Small Water, is enlivened by the sight of mountain bikers toiling up the path, their bikes slung over one shoulder, who, once they reach the top, come haring down again over the rough fellside. The pattern is for them to ride for a few hundred yards until forced to stop, either voluntarily to repair the bike, or involuntarily when they crash. After a pause they start again, ignoring the blood streaming from their knees and elbows.

Small Water sits at the bottom, perfectly cupped in the hand of the mountain. The beck running out of it is a good place to bathe tired, overheated feet.

The view over Small Water towards Haweswater, seen from Nan Bield Pass

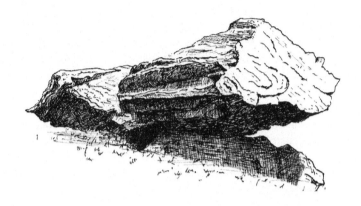

This rock is near Small Water; it appears to have been neatly sawn off and resembles a large piece of beef

Ullswater

'Lovely' is the adjective often used to describe Ullswater, and it is exactly right. If you approach from the north down the little road from Dockray, just as you round a bend there is a sudden view of the lake and the mountains beyond it that is simply jaw-dropping – surely one of the most beautiful views anywhere in England, a country blessed with a great many to choose from.

This loveliness leads to a romantic turn of mind that the tourist industry has been quick to exploit, and brochures issued by some of the local businesses do more than hint at a link between Ullswater and the legend of King Arthur. In fact, although they don't say so directly, you could come away with the impression that this is indeed where the mysterious lady of the lake gave the sword Excalibur to a young King Arthur and where, many years later, as the king lay dying from his wounds, Sir Bedivere very reluctantly threw it back.

It is a legend with roots that go back to a distant past; a pre-Christian, pagan past where rivers and lakes had gods who could be appeased or bargained with by sacrificing objects of great value, objects that represented significant investment of labour, artistic endeavour and wealth: weapons, jewellery, goblets, coins. It is an idea that still has an emotional pull even today, the sense that our lives are closely bound up in some way with forces here on the earth, not with some disembodied god 'out there', and in a way, given that we have evolved over vast chasms of time in a close wrestle with soil, water and air, it has more truth in it than might first appear. So if you ever find yourself with the need to cast a war-battered jewel-encrusted kingly sword out onto the waters, Ullswater is undoubtedly the best place in England to do it (but it's probably wise not to let the local tourist business know about it).

The southern end of Ullswater: possibly the most beautiful view in England. This was drawn while sitting on the hillside just off the Dockray road.

Aira Force

Just off the Dockray road is another famous site: Aira Force. This waterfall, with a drop of 65 feet, is deeply embedded in the forested side of the fell. There are paths that weave their way through the trees, crossing the falls via an arched stone bridge. At the bottom it's possible to get close to where the water splashes into an echoing rocky basin, a natural fairy-land grotto, heavily decorated with thick green moss and ferns.

Aira Force

Unfortunately, walking on Ullswater's north shore is not so easy because of the road that clings to the edge of the lake, although there are short and pleasant walks higher up the fellside, such as to the memorial seat, a well-built seat crafted from stone, from where the views over the lake are very beautiful. There are more possibilities on the opposite shore, however, where there is an excellent and easy walk along the shore to Howtown, from where you can get the steamer back to Glenridding.

This was drawn on the spot, sitting on the lakeside on the promontory that leads out to the ferry jetty near Glenridding.

The lake-shore path to Howtown is full of variety, passing over rocky hillocks and through chaotic woods. This fallen tree almost blocks the path, and has rocks embedded in it.

One of the lake-side paths passes behind Silver Crag, in a little valley. On emerging, a wide view over the lake to the north suddenly opens up.

Helvellyn via Striding Edge

Few things beat the feeling you get setting out early on a fine morning with a full day's walking ahead of you. There are scarcely any people about, the sky is clear and blue, the air is bracing, and the only sounds are the perpetual gurgling of water, the twitter of birds and the far-off bleating of sheep. Your boots are still dry and warm, blisters are at bay and your legs feel strong. Your stride is longer, bolder, than back in the city streets at home, and you feel bravely confident as you walk up the lane looking for the gate or stile that will lead off to your chosen fell.

The feeling might not last to the end of the day, but let's hold on to it for now, and set out from Patterdale, walking through the little village past the oddly shaped White Lion Inn, positioned by its builders 200 years ago at the roadside with no thought given to the future requirements of cars which now have to squeeze through the narrow pinch-point between it and the buildings opposite. Walking north towards Ullswater you pass some meadows and the George Starkey mountain hut (on the roadside, not on a mountain), then a peaceful slate-built church and the old police station. Then, just before the bridge over Grisedale Beck, the way turns left up a signposted lane.

This lane twists along for half a mile or so in deep green quietude, rising gradually so that Grisedale Beck eventually re-appears at the bottom of a steep wooded slope on the right-hand side. Finally you clear the woods and reach a point where you turn sharp right to cross the beck and begin the climb up Birkhouse Moor.

As you rise, a view of the valley of Grisedale opens up, with the grand sweep of the southern end of the Helvellyn range in the distance, and the day's work to come. Grisedale is about two miles long; a wide, flat-bottomed valley bounded by St Sunday Crag on the south, Birkhouse Moor, Bleaberry Crag and the distant crags above Patterdale Common on the north. Although Helvellyn cannot be seen from here, the far-off view of its adjoining fells is quite spectacular, and worth delaying over for a few minutes.

Grisedale, seen from Birkhouse Moor

The ascent up the flank of Birkhouse Moor is one of those things that just has to be done; there is no point in grumbling. The contours are close together, but the path is angled upwards rather than full-on, and there is plenty of scenery to look at. There is a sort of interval, where the way levels off for a while, before another line of ascent up to the top of the ridge, a wall and its hole.

All routes up to Striding Edge converge at Hole-in-the-Wall. It's the point where it really becomes possible to see Helvellyn and the start of the route along Striding Edge. Red Tarn lies below in the twin-armed embrace of

Striding Edge and Swirral Edge, with Catstye Cam standing on sentry duty over on the far side.

Immediately after Hole-in-the-Wall the path rises over Bleaberry Crag, which is moderately rough but nothing more, and just as you might be wondering what all the fuss is about, Striding Edge comes into full view.

Striding Edge

Striding Edge is a sharp rock edge, with precipitous slopes on either side. It's a jagged edge too, rising and falling like a row of bad teeth from a giant carnivore. For much of its length it's possible to walk along the very top where the edge is flattened to a width of two or three feet, but this requires a degree of nerve and good balance, and the rocks have been polished smooth by constant use. If that is too daunting there are other paths a little lower down on the north side that allow a greater sense of security yet still provide an exhilarating scramble, often requiring full use of fingers and toes.

So long as the weather is good and you take your time, Striding Edge is demanding but safe. At busy times there are queues of people making their way along, and although there are some accidents, their numbers are few in relation to the thousands who safely get across every year. Only at the end, as you reach the slopes of Helvellyn, is there a point where there may be some difficulty: a rock chimney that has to be climbed down. Its difficulty is exaggerated, I would say, and, just as on the rest of the way, patience and careful thought about where to put hands and feet will conquer it. (However, if you happen to be a dog it's a different matter.)

Striding Edge is something special, to be savoured, although I often find its ascent is over in what seems like a very short time. Maybe that's an illusion caused by the intense mental focus the task requires. Anyway, having done it once you're unlikely to forget the experience. It has its obvious dangers, so it's a walk for fine days: strong winds, fog, ice or heavy rain rule it out for most of us.

With Striding Edge safely crossed, there is a scramble up a steep slope of jagged rocks that look a bit intimidating at first but which are, in fact, quite easy to climb. Then there's a short run up the final rounded slope to the summit from where you can look back at the path you just took with deserved satisfaction.

Striding Edge, seen from above

At this point, Swirral Edge deserves a few words. If it wasn't for its bigger brother to the south, Swirral Edge would be famous in its own right as a perilous ascent that strikes fear into the heart, etc etc. It's shorter than Striding Edge, but much steeper, and just as sharp-edged. It can be seen clearly from Hole-in-the-Wall, part of the craggy outline traced from Helvellyn over to Catstye Cam. The route to it starts from Red Tarn, via a very obvious path that curves above the tarn straight up to the edge.

I came to Swirral late, for, like many visitors with restricted time, the temptation was always to use the most exciting route, imagining that I would try the other another time. So it was relatively recently that I climbed Swirral Edge, on a clear, cold day. On reaching the arête a wide view opens up to the north across the dramatic basin of Brown Cove, but there isn't much leisure time to enjoy it because this path is steep and badly eroded, so concentration is required. The steepest part entails 80 metres of ascent at a gradient approaching 0.7. Wainwright likened it to a rock staircase, but this was not my experience. There are so many tracks laid down by people trying to avoid the erosion that the choice is bewildering, and I struggled up a crumbling path to the left of the edge, wondering how wise this was. Clinging on with my face pressed close to the ground, I saw that the surface was scattered with grass seed. How sobering: here was I making all this fuss while someone had been here earlier sowing the soil with seed to try to reverse the damage I was unwittingly causing.

From either route up, Red Tarn is always visible far below. One of the highest tarns in the Lake District, at 2,355 feet (718 metres), it has a bleak aspect to it, even in good weather, cradled in a ring of rocky crags and slopes; in winter it thickly freezes over. Although it looks natural, like so much of the Lake District it has been shaped in part by man. Close to its shores is a strange stone-built channel, dry now, and appearing to slope the wrong way for carrying water out of the tarn, yet this is part of a system built in the 19th century to supply water to the Greenside lead mine in Glenridding valley. Now it is derelict and the waters have breached the old dam. There are fish in Red Tarn, maybe: references mostly say the tarn 'is said to contain' schelly – a rare freshwater fish otherwise found only in Brothers Water, Haweswater and Ullswater. Truly, a local species.

Helvellyn seen from the shores of Red Tarn

The top of Helvellyn is surprisingly flat, rolling away in long, broad, curves, northwards towards Raise and Stybarrow Dodd, and southwards in a direct line over Nethermost Pike and Dollywagon Pike. It looks just like an enormous aerial golf course. There's an old Ordnance Survey trig point to mark the summit, but most people make a bee-line for the stone shelter, built in the form of a cross with a seat running around the inside of the wall, so there's a chance you'll find somewhere to sit out of the wind – unless it's already crowded with visitors – to be pestered by sheep that have discovered a liking for sandwiches. You're likely to find cyclists up here too, taking advantage of the smooth profile of the summits; this might come as a surprise, but not all routes up are as arduous as the one you just took.

The views are extensive, and as you explore the top, you will almost certainly come across a memorial plaque marking the day that an aeroplane landed here. This is one of three memorials on Helvellyn; you might have noticed the other two already.

Memorial 1: The Dixon memorial. This is the most easily missed of the three. It's an iron plaque on a post standing on an outcrop of rock on the south side of Striding Edge, and it marks the spot where Robert Dixon fell to his death in 1858 while 'following the Patterdale foxhounds'.

Memorial 2: This is a stone slab which reads: 'The first aeroplane to land on a mountain in Great Britain did so on this spot on December 22nd 1922. John Leeming and Bert Hinkler in an Avro 585 Gosport landed here and after a short stay flew back to Woodford.' It's the 'after a short stay flew back to Woodford' that amuses me. So they turned up, looked around a bit, decided there wasn't much to be done here and went home.

Memorial 3: The Gough memorial. This is probably the most famous of the three, and is certainly the biggest – a large stone slab set in a mounting on the top slopes of the fell just below the rim. It commemorates a story good enough to spend a few moments relating it.

On the 17th April 1805 Charles Gough, a young artist from Manchester, set out from Patterdale to climb Striding Edge. He never returned.

Some three months later his body was found where he had fallen. It was clear that he had slipped from the Edge to his death, but to everyone's astonishment, there, still with him, was his faithful dog, standing guard over the body.

The story soon hit the newspapers, and a reading public ready for tales of loyalty and duty eagerly bought it. What hardships the dog must have endured! What endurance in the face of the storms! What devotion it had shown! If a dumb beast could behave like this, what should be expected of a people mired in the Napoleonic wars? Wordsworth and Scott wrote poems about it, and a few years later Landseer painted a mawkish picture of the scene in which the loyal mutt sadly paws a rather healthy looking corpse wrapped in a blanket with its limbs artfully disposed for dramatic effect.

But behind all this there was one awkward question that only the gutter-press of the day had the nerve to ask. During all its sufferings and hardships, what, exactly, had the dog been eating?

It's a strange name, Helvellyn. With its 'llyn' ending it looks and sounds Welsh, as if it was mislaid by a Welsh poet. It certainly has associations with English poetry: Wordsworth was a regular visitor, and there is a portrait of him in the National Portrait Gallery in which he stands on Helvellyn, looking sombre and dignified, his eyes cast downwards. Once he climbed it with Humphry Davy, the chemist, and Sir Walter Scott. It was just after Charles Gough's accident, and both Wordsworth and Scott wrote their poems about the event afterwards.

But, to return to business. The view north-south is of a golf links, and to the west there are steep rounded descents to Thirlmere, not visible from the summit, but to the east it is a spectacularly rough and rugged scene over Striding Edge and Swirral. Swirral offers a way down, often used to make a circular route back down to Red Tarn, or over to Catstye Cam. Having worked so hard to get to the top it seems a pity to come down immediately, and so the southern route beckons.

The path is broad and clear, leading due south from the point above

Striding Edge. For some reason it drifts off to the west, following the smooth contours of Helvellyn's humped back, away from the ridge's edge. That might suit the mountain bikers, but it means you miss all the best views, so unless it's misty, keep a few hundred yards to the east so you can peer down into Nethermost Cove and admire the long promontory jutting out from Nethermost Pike over Grisedale, which is now far below. The top of Nethermost Pike is broad and flat and covered in rocks, many of them standing on edge, sharply chiselled, as if they were set there by ancient worshippers of the sun and moon, but really it's because of the way the tilted rocks have been eroded over millions of years.

Sharp, jagged stones on Nethermost Pike. This is something of a fieldmouse's view: the stones are mostly about eighteen inches high.

Next comes High Crag, above another gaping chasm leading down to Grisedale, and then the fell with the oddest name in the whole Lake District: Dollywaggon Pike. This is the last peak in the ridge, and like the others it's wild and rugged on the east, rounded and dull on the west. Perhaps to compensate for their dullness the lower slopes have another notable name: Willie Wife Moor. Both names hint at the stories of lives once lived and now forgotten, but their true origins are mysteries.

The broad skirts of Willie Wife Moor sweep around the south end of Dollywaggon Pike, and the main path down runs down those slopes to Grisedale Tarn.

Not so long ago this path was a miserable affair. Heavily used for access to and from Helvellyn it was in a poor state of decline, difficult and even dangerous to walk on, with loose stones and earth everywhere, an ever-widening scar on the fellside. Now, after much artful labour, it is quite a marvel. Not only has the path been reconstructed, but it has been done in a way that hardly looks artificial at all; rather it has the appearance of a natural arrangement of colossal rocks that just happen to be perfectly suited for walking on. It's a great success and gift to walkers.

I like Grisedale Tarn. It's on a busy crossroads of paths, quite large, surrounded by towering fells, and after struggling down from Dollywaggon Pike on a hot day its cold clear waters are tempting. Its outflow is from the north-east corner, flowing into Grisedale; passing this way once I saw the shallow stream was full of hundreds of tiny baby brown trout enjoying the warmth of the sun.

The tarn has older associations too. Somewhere in its depths lies the crown of the last king of Cumbria, thrown there by his defeated soldiers as they fled from the battle of Dunmail Raise. Naturally, the warriors return each year as ghosts to reclaim the crown from the waters. And then, a little to the north-east on the path into Grisedale valley, is the Brothers' Parting Stone, which marks the place where Wordsworth parted with his brother John, who was on his way to join a ship and go to sea. John drowned in 1805 when his ship sank off the coast of Dorset. The stone has some lines of poetry on it, but they are pretty much illegible now, weathered away.

The path beside the tarn's outflow is the way back to Patterdale, along the floor of the valley, although anyone who still has energy to use might dash up St Sunday Crag to follow its ridge. However, the valley route has much to be said for it, and avoids more hard work for tired leg muscles.

Waterfalls in Grisedale, behind Ruthwaite Lodge climbing hut

Greenside Mine

Looking over Ullswater towards the Glenridding valley. The mine is high up the valley. (Drawn on the spot.)

There is a rough track leading up from Glenridding, the Greenside Road, that follows the beck as far as the youth hostel. All around the hostel and up the valley beyond it are the tell-tale signs of mining activity, for this was once the site of the Greenside lead mines.

Mining here began in the 17th century, but it reached its peak in the mid-19th century, when the mine was producing both lead and silver. Most of the silver was sent to the Royal Mint, but the lead was put to many uses, and it is said that some of it was made into bullets used in the American Civil War. In the early days the work was mostly manual, but as the operation grew and the depth of the mines necessarily increased, more mechanisation was introduced. Red Tarn, below Helvellyn, was dammed in the 1840s, and the Keppel Cove dam was built in the 1860s, in both cases to provide water for the mine to power mills and smelting gear. Towards the end of the century the water was used to generate electricity to power the mining equipment; Greenside Mine was always technically advanced for its time.

However, the mine had its troubles. In 1862 there was a massive rock fall, known as 'the Big Crush'. It was estimated that 110,000 tons of rock fell, and it took four years to clear. Then in 1927 the Keppel Cove dam burst, causing massive flooding and destruction in Glenridding. A new dam was built in concrete, but it failed in 1931, albeit less disastrously. Later, in 1952, a serious underground fire killed four men.

As the seams were worked out, the depth of the operations increased, and by the end of the Second World War the mine workings extended to a depth of 400 metres, making them ideal for an unexpected role in 1959. At that time negotiations were being held with the Russians to agree a nuclear test ban. Any ban would only be viable if it could be verified, but there was a suspicion that it might be possible to disguise underground nuclear tests by, in effect, muffling them. Known as decoupling, the idea was that if the blast took place in a large chamber, rather than packed into solid rock, the shock waves would be substantially suppressed, making it almost impossible for remote seismic monitors to detect them. So in late 1959 men from the Atomic Weapons Research Establishment arrived to make preparations for two test blasts – one coupled and another, much larger, de-coupled. They didn't use nuclear explosives, of course, but they detonated over 4,000 pounds of TNT and showed that the decoupling theory was correct: it was possible to conceal an underground blast. The result was that underground tests were excluded from the ratified test ban treaty and remain so today.

The mine didn't survive long after that as world lead prices fell while the costs of extraction rose, and it finally closed in 1961. Many of the buildings were demolished, with the few that survived being converted to outdoor centres.

A little beyond the Youth Hostel lie those remaining buildings, and up on the right-hand side there is Swart Beck, strewn with the wreckage of the old mining buildings and with piles of spoil heaped up alongside; a scene of ruin that is an eyesore even now, more than half a century after it all closed.

Swart Beck and the ruined mine buildings

It is possible to walk up among the ruins – it's actually the way to Stick's Pass – and although the more dangerous areas are fenced off, the track snakes its way up so you get a sense of the substantial scale of the operation. The machinery has gone of course, except for some immovable items, such as enigmatic pieces of rusting steel, still bolted into the rock.

Little remains of the old machinery, except for fragments that were firmly bolted into the rock

This looks like an old-fashioned birdcage, but it is actually a cover over the top of a shaft

This is a view from the path up Swart Beck, looking down Glenridding valley. The spoil heap, contaminated with lead, is largely grassed over now, but that flat top, smooth enough for a cricket pitch, and those neatly sloping sides, betray its artificial origins.

Old ruins can be found all the way up the beck, including at one point a weir. If you continue the ascent, passing a little forest of yew trees, you eventually reach a wide flattish basin, with Green Side – the fell, not the mine – curving around in the distance. There's a wooden footbridge, and it is striking how the ground underfoot here is sandy grit, like nothing else in the area, presumably another consequence of the mining. This place is rather desolate, with long fingers of huge boulders piled up transversely in front of you; you can climb up on top and walk along them, pondering how they got there. They certainly don't look like they arrived naturally. A clue might lie high above on the right, where there are two gaping holes in the fellside. They look like long-abandoned quarries and are labelled as such on the OS map, but in fact this is where the great crush of 1862 happened, and the holes are the result of the collapse of the mine; fortunately it happened on a Sunday, when no one was there. Sticks Pass can be seen following the contours below Green Side in a long arc around the basin, with little heaps of moraine dotted about in the distance. If you look very carefully to the west you can just make out a small building, a hut, all alone on the hillside. Look more closely and beside the hut there is something else, a row of towers climbing the slopes of Raise: it's a ski-tow, and the hut is a ski-hut.

An old weir above the main Greenside complex

Back down at the old mine workings, a broad track leads to the Keppel Cove dam. It's surprisingly large, charcoal grey, with a great hole roughly hacked through it where it was deliberately breached before its final abandonment. A stream runs through the gap – a modest trickle that gives no clue as to the volume of water once held back here. You get a sense of that if you continue past the dam to Keppel Cove itself, over to the right somewhat, embraced by steep crags. Empty now, it's easy to see that this could once have held a large reservoir, and to imagine the scale of the disaster that followed the first dam's failure in 1927.

The breached Keppel Cove dam. Website blogs have photographs of people standing on the dam's top edge, which is about five feet wide, but access is fenced off and notice boards carry stern warnings to keep off. There is no hand rail.

Keep going beyond the dam and you soon reach Brown Cove, where there is yet another dam, much smaller than Keppel Cove's. Brown Cove dam was built of stone in 1860, also to serve the Greenside mine, but now it too is breached, and the tarn behind it – another creation of the mining company – is little more than a small pool. However, its setting is grand, surrounded by the curved walls of Whiteside, Helvellyn, Swirral Edge and Catstye Cam.

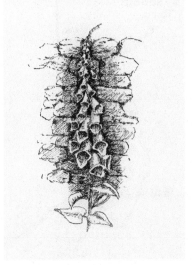

Thirlmere

It was as long ago as the 1850s that Manchester Corporation first set its eyes on the Lake District as a source of fresh drinking water for its expanding population. Thirlmere was not the first lake to be considered – Ullswater and Haweswater had already been rejected – but after much wrangling and argument, and in the face of huge local opposition, Royal Assent to a parliamentary bill to dam Thirlmere was granted in 1879.

It wasn't called Thirlmere before then but Wythburn Water, or sometimes Leathes Water, and it was close to being divided into two lakes by a pair of narrow peninsulas that almost met in the middle and which were joined by a bridge. Converting Wythburn Water to a reservoir was a huge engineering project that entailed building a dam, and a tunnel under Dunmail Raise, while such stone constructions as were visible were built in a mock medieval style, much the fashion in those days. The reservoir was finally declared open on October the 13th 1894, when water was carried all the way to Albert Square in Manchester where there was a proud opening ceremony.

Possibly what caused the longest lasting resentment about Thirlmere was that because the water was not treated the Corporation decided that to protect its purity all public access to its shores should be prohibited. Further, the engineers advised that the lake shores should be planted with trees to stabilise the soil and prevent run-off. This was done, but with a large plantation of non-native fir trees. Thirlmere was lost twice: first by the prohibition of public access and second by hiding it behind artificial forests.

This is how I remember Thirlmere in my youth, the whole lake being off-limits, visible only in brief glimpses through the trees as you drove up the A591 between Grasmere and Keswick – a road for which, incidentally, we have the reservoir engineers to thank. It wasn't until 1989 that Thirlmere got a water treatment plant, which meant that restrictions on public access could be relaxed, and you can now walk along the shore, or drive along the narrow winding road on the western side. Thirlmere is now owned and managed by a company called United Utilities – a name of provoking blandness, revealing nothing about what it does. What it does is manage water supplies in the North West: both Thirlmere and Haweswater are in its care, along with many smaller waters.

Even though memories are fading, books are still written about the imposition of Thirlmere on the people of Cumbria; a classic confrontation between city and country. Yet the enormous engineering achievement that it was is seldom mentioned. The dam at the north end stands 65 feet above the old stream bed – no mean achievement in itself – but what seems even more extraordinary is the aqueduct that carries the water 96 miles to Manchester. Designed to carry 55 million gallons of water per day, it passes under

Dunmail Raise, then to the north of Windermere, over to Kendal, and all the way south to the great city, yet it is so well concealed that no visitor to the Lakes would ever be aware of it. Moreover, no pumping stations were required because, falling an average of 20 inches per mile, its flow is entirely governed by gravity.

It is curious to ponder on this and reflect that the clean and pure water that Manchester sought, running off the fellsides into the lake, no longer finds its way back to the sea via Cumbria's babbling brooks and rivers but via the sewers and drains of Manchester.

Despite all the controversy of the past, I think you would have to be wilfully blind and stubborn not to recognise that Thirlmere is now quite beautiful. Sure, it has the ugly scoured shoreline of a man-made reservoir, caused by the water rising and falling, and there are many, many spruce trees still there, but there are areas fenced off from sheep, and a broader mix of woodland is appearing as a result. Many of these are actively managed by United Utilities, such as at Launchy Gill, where the Gill tumbles down a rocky waterfall in a landscape thick with rich mosses and ferns and 'natural' woodland thought to be close to how the area might have looked before it was deforested. Nearby, there is this:

Tottling Stone

This huge boulder, at least four metres high, stands very improbably balanced on the brink of a steep hill, perched so precariously that daylight passes underneath it. No doubt geologists will have a rational explanation for how it came to be here, but for most of us the reaction has to be one of incomprehension; the puzzle isn't just how it came to be there but why it didn't roll down the slope long ago. Maybe it will, one day: the little car park at the bottom of the Gill is right in its path[15].

---

[15] There is a photograph of the rock taken in the 1890s, showing it standing entirely clear of spruce trees high above Wythburn Water, with the old bridge over the lake clearly visible. There are many references to it online, such as this: http://www.geog.port.ac.uk/webmap/thelakes/large/hb0919.jpg

Grasmere

The big attraction here is William Wordsworth's house, Dove Cottage. For years I couldn't bring myself to visit it, to join the procession of faintly bored tourists trooping in and out every day to enjoy whatever transforming experience it is that they undergo as they gaze at the bedroom he slept in or the chair he might have sat in. Wordsworth's true monument is his poetry, I would think to myself; look for him there, not in the gift shop's range of printed tea towels and mugs. However, I contradicted myself, for I've visited Ruskin's house several times – not that I ever bought a tea towel – and it's only half convincing to say that Ruskin's paintings have to be seen in the flesh, while old Wudsworth wasn't known for his watercolours.

All rubbish, of course. Eventually I did visit the house and it is excellent. The cottage, which had been a pub immediately before Wordsworth rented it, is tiny, and groups of visitors are taken around by a well-informed guide. Nearby there's a museum so interesting that I visited it twice.

Wordsworth lived here for eight years, sharing the house with his sister Dorothy until he married and moved down the road to Rydal Mount, overlooking Rydal Water, where he stayed for the rest of his life. He came from a well-to-do background, and lived a long and fairly modest life, tracing the path that so many have done before and since, from fiery young radical writing poems in praise of the French revolution and even of Napoleon (both were only temporary enthusiasms) to a rather staid conservatism of later years – at one stage actively supporting the local Tory party candidate for Parliament. He led a slightly comical double life, on the one hand as the famous poet who wrote more eloquently and movingly about the beauty of the natural world and the power it can have over human consciousness than anyone had done before, and on the other as the Distributor of Stamps for Westmorland. Poetry's all very well, but it's no way to pay the bills, and his second job provided the necessary income as he struggled to make his name as a poet while raising a young family.

This was all very different to his friend Samuel Taylor Coleridge, a much more conflicted and flawed character. Coleridge lived for three years at Greta Hall in Keswick, and the two men collaborated on *Lyrical Ballads*, in which they developed a radically new form of poetry, ditching the rather pompous declamatory style of the late 18th century that they felt had become formulaic and dead, and writing in language much closer to how people actually spoke. It was the birth of English Romantic poetry. But while Wordsworth's career seemed to progress onwards and upwards, albeit after a slow start, Coleridge's life was one of struggle, anxiety and disappointment. He felt overshadowed by Wordsworth, believing that his friend possessed the greater poetic talent, and his self-doubt must have been worsened later when he received savage reviews of poems such as 'Christabel'. There was his failed marriage and the frustration of his affair with his real love, Sara Hutchinson; he more or less abandoned his wife and family, while his son Hartley – about whom, when an infant, Coleridge had written so movingly, deeming it 'wise to make him Nature's play-mate' in the belief that this would make the boy grow up to be a good and happy adult – turned out bad, drinking heavily and walking out of Coleridge's life for good at the age of 26, leaving the older man standing blinking at the roadside in London. And most famously there was his notorious and lifelong struggle with opium, to which he first became addicted through taking it as laudanum, widely used in those days for medical treatment. (There is a suspicion that his addiction was fed by an unscrupulous doctor.)

For all that, Coleridge's 'Rime of the Ancient Mariner' has surely made a deeper and longer-lasting impression on the national consciousness than just about anything Wordsworth wrote, and that includes the daffodils poem – for which, incidentally, Wordsworth was cruelly mocked by the critics of his day.

As for Dove Cottage, when Wordsworth moved out he handed the tenancy over to Thomas de Quincey, another literary giant of the time, best known now for *Confessions of an English Opium Eater*; yes, he too was an addict, falling victim, like Coleridge, after taking the drug on medical advice. De Quincey lived there for 12 years, but continued to rent the cottage after moving out, using it to store books. Later he returned to Rydal, sharing Nab Cottage with Hartley Coleridge.

Wordsworth wrote that Grasmere is 'The loveliest spot that man hath ever known'. All visitors come to know this because it's written in curly-script letters on a board outside the Wordsworth Hotel. The village certainly does have charm, but these days it's a place of large hotels serving 'luncheon' and afternoon teas, of crocodile lines of tourists being led from the coach park to Wordsworth's grave in the churchyard, and overweight gents in t-shirts wandering around looking overheated and wondering how to fill in the time between luncheon and dinner.

Despite all that, where tourists gather there is usually good cause, and this is true of Grasmere. St Oswald's church, which looks drab from the outside, being rather squat and covered in rough grey rendering, is a revelation inside. Large and airy, with whitewashed walls and a beamed roof, parts of it date from 1250, and it contains many memorials, including Wordsworth's. The Wordsworth family grave is in the churchyard outside, surrounded by large yew trees, eight of them planted by Wordsworth himself. Nearby is the grave of William Green, a local artist and illustrator from the early 19th century, who was based in Ambleside.

And there are many other things: the river and the meadows, the Heaton Cooper Studio, even the Youth Hostel is striking – a large 19th-century slate-built mansion standing in its own grounds on the north side of the town. But best of all are the lake and the surrounding fells.

Unfortunately not all of the lake shore is accessible, particularly at the north end, by the village. However, a walk along the quiet road on the west side, itself a demonstration of how man and nature can work together so well in the lakes, with water dripping through mossy stone walls, ferns in abundance and a green canopy overhead, quickly brings you to a path that runs down to the shore. Loughrigg Terrace runs across the gently rising fellside at the southern end of the lake, from which can be seen one of the most famous views in the area: over the lake to Grasmere village, Helm Crag and the unmistakable hollowed-out dip of the pass at Dunmail Raise.

The view over Grasmere from Loughrigg Terrace

Helm Crag

This little fell is on every coach driver's commentary script, requiring him to draw his sleepy passengers' attention to the Lion and the Lamb up on the summit. And indeed there is a strong likeness, one larger clump of rocks playing the part of the lion, and a smaller bobble next to it the lamb. They are best seen from the east side – from the main road in fact, much to the coach drivers' advantage.

Helm Crag, with the Lion and the Lamb

The crag provides a popular walk, and with good reason, for in the span of about forty minutes' ascent it yields grassy paths, rocky paths, an old quarry, a steep built-up path, woods, a little rocky gorge, extensive views and rocky scrambles at the top. Enjoyable for any walker, it is a perfect introduction to the fells for children, encompassing nearly all the experiences one would find on larger climbs, all within an ascent of 1,100 feet from Grasmere village. Indeed, for variety and enjoyment Helm Crag surpasses many of its bigger neighbours, who are exposed as lumbering country bumpkins by comparison with this lively, witty little fell.

From the village the route follows the Easdale Road to the north-west, skirting the broad flat meadows through which Easedale Beck flows. At Brimmer Head Farm there is a signposted path to the right, and from there the route is obvious. There are some new path sections to replace older ones damaged by erosion, and one very steep section up a built path, but no difficulties, while in good weather it would take wayward stubbornness to get lost.

There are more surprises once the summit is reached, for there are two candidates for that honour, one at each end of a ridge. The first is the lion of said lion plus lamb, but a short distance away there's another candidate, known, for reasons that are immediately obvious, as the Howitzer. The Lion and Lamb's appearance from the valley can be understood more clearly from up here; the lion is a rounded protuberance of rock that might not have attracted half so much attention were it not for its companion, the chunk of rock sticking up next to it with a convincing likeness of a small animal's head on its top. The lion is easily climbed, but while standing on its skull you're fooling yourself if you think you've reached the highest point, because that, in fact, is on top of the Howitzer. This offers a quite different challenge, for it needs some rock-climbing skills to conquer it, and few of the Helm's visitors manage to do that; not many even try, although plenty make a half-hearted attempt for the sake of appearances and the camera.

The Howitzer has other names, including the Lion Couchant (really?) and, even less probably, The Old Lady Playing the Organ. Sorry madam, but if those rocks resemble anything, it's an old-fashioned Howitzer.

The ridge between these two rocky termini is about 250 yards long and strewn with boulders. There is a deep depression running along its length with a second, lower ridge beyond it: at some time in the far-off past the north-east face of the fell broke away and slipped downhill, leaving this confused rough jumble of rocks.

Helm Crag can be linked to longer walks by following the long ridge to Greenup Edge, but somehow it doesn't seem necessary. The fell provides a perfect walk for a summer evening, and a return to Grasmere by the same route with the lake spread out before you will not disappoint. If accompanied by intrepid young children they will happily tear off ahead, beating you to the bottom.

The Howitzer

Easedale

This is another easy but rewarding walk, with a long pedigree: it was once a favourite of William and Dorothy Wordsworth. It leaves the Easedale Road by a signposted path, immediately crossing Easedale beck and then following a pleasant route over the meadows, with the beck on the right. In its early stages the path is made of broad flat stones, clearly recycled from some older use, while the beck is deep and clear, inviting you to stand for a few minutes, gazing into it.

Eventually the climb starts. The path is rough in places, but this is a favourite tourist route and nowhere is it at all difficult. There's a good view of the Sourmilk Gill waterfalls tumbling down Ecton Crag – the only steep part of the walk – followed by a duller flattish stretch, after which Easedale Tarn is reached.

Moonlight on Easedale Tarn

Rydal Water

Despite the busy main road that runs along its northern shore, and the coach parties and all the rest of them that gather here, Rydal Water is a lovely place, with charming easy walks on its shores below fells that you can admire on days when your legs just don't seem to want to do any hard work. I have two special memories of Rydal Water: it was the first lake I remember seeing frozen solid, one cold January day; it's also where my sons used to go fishing for pike. Rydal is home to many pike – a source of much fun for young lads, but less so for the warden who happened to pass by and whose opinion about the lake hosting so many voracious predators seemed to be that he hoped my sons would catch them all and take them away.

Rydal Water seen from White Moss, the headland that separates
Rydal water and Grasmere

After leaving Grasmere, Wordsworth settled at Rydal Mount, in the tiny village of Rydal. One of his favourite walks was under Nab Scar, the rough fellside to the north of the lake. His judgement was, as ever in these matters, quite right. The path is still there, and it is a delight, passing through woods, with glimpses of the lake through the trees and rich springy moss on the rocks. It is no less delightful for knowing that it's called the coffin trail; at one time St Oswald's in Grasmere was the only church in the area with a consecrated burial ground, so the dead had to be brought – carried – from as far as Ambleside to be buried. You can still find stone benches at intervals along the path, provided to lay the body on while the bearers paused to rest.

Grasmere and Rydal Water are connected by a short stretch of river, and their joint appearance on maps has always reminded me of an anatomical drawing of a small mammal's digestive system.

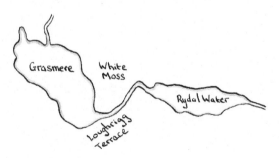

Rydal Cave

This enormous cave – actually an old slate quarry – is right next to the main path running along the southern shore of Rydal Water. It is partly flooded, so those who venture in will almost certainly get water-filled boots, but people do splash into its green-blue hall, which echoes with the plopping of dripping water. There are even stepping stones to help them along. On the other hand there have been reports of large lumps of rock falling from the ceiling, so no responsible guidebook would ever recommend entering.

Rydal Cave; in fact it's a disused quarry

9 WASTWATER AND THE HIGH CENTRAL FELLS

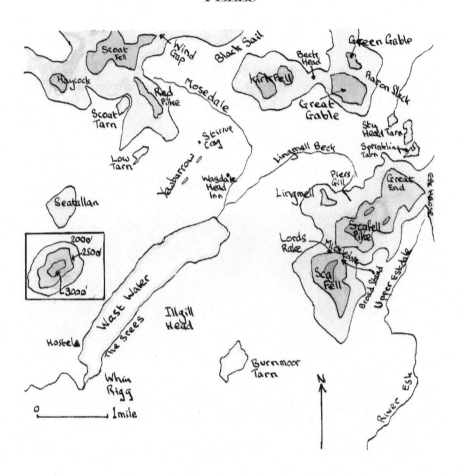

Wastwater Screes

When I was a small child living in Cockermouth, Wastwater was a favourite place for family visits on sunny Sunday afternoons so we could marvel at the Wastwater Screes. They seem to come screaming down to the lakeside almost vertically, fanning out in great sweeping arcs as they tumble from the crumbling rocks and crags at the top. And their journey doesn't stop at the water's edge: at 258 feet (79 metres) Wastwater is England's deepest lake, and the screes plunge into the water to continue their journey far down into its icy depths.

It seems natural to write about the screes as if they were in perpetual, restless, motion, for they look like a flowing mass, but they aren't really. Or rather they are, but on a much longer timescale than short-lived mortals experience. Sitting on the opposite shore you hear from time to time the distant clatter of a rock as it breaks free and tumbles down the slopes, adding its small contribution to a geological process that has gone on for millions of years. Nature has time to spare – and lots of it.

The screes often take on a very sombre appearance, grey and hostile, but in the evening when the setting sun catches them they become flooded with golden light, glinting and shimmering for a few minutes until the night's shadows fall.

The Wastwater Screes

Just as the screes are not quite in permanent flowing motion, neither are they quite vertical, but they come close. The top of Illgill Head, their highest point, is 520 metres above the water surface, with its face making an average angle to the horizontal of 70 degrees. So it is perhaps surprising to find that it's possible to walk along the scree, following a path along the water's edge. Even better, this path can be linked to a walk along the top of the crags, creating a circular route full of dramatic scenery.

The screes lie on the faces of two fells: Whin Rigg and Illgill Head. One way to tackle them starts at the south-west end of the lake, using a very steep path that follows Greathall Gill, itself an impressive sight. The start of the path may take some seeking out; the last time I used it there was much disruption caused by construction of a new pipeline to take water from the lake to Sellafield nuclear power station. A very attractive approach is from the Youth Hostel, following the shore around Low Wood and crossing the River Irt via the Lund Bridge. The woods are peaceful, while the views across the lake past the screes to Great Gable are spectacular – unless, of course the weather allows you to see nothing more than a grey wet haze.

The view across Wastwater towards Great Gable

The ascent is short and sharp, rising very steeply until it rounds off to a gentler slope up to the summit of Whin Rigg. From here it can be seen, as so often happens, that both Whin Rigg and Illgill Head have dual personalities, offering profoundly dramatic and challenging scenery on one side, above Wastwater, but a timid and dull appearance on the other, with little more than featureless slopes of grass, heather and bracken gently rolling down to Miterdale. Not that the slopes leading to Miterdale are why most people will be up here. While the main path seems to keep rather too far to the right, away from the edge, there is a smaller path that takes you where you really want to be, right above the crags and gullies from which the screes were born.

The views from here are quite special. Huge clefts open up in the crags, down which it's possible to peer right down to the water 500 metres below. There is a sequence of them, one after another as you progress along the top, each of them likely to induce a feeling of dizziness from the height and the thrill of danger, given the obviously merciless consequences should you fall into one of them. (It need hardly be said that the danger is real enough, and the gullies are not to be entered. People have died here. In mist it's probably wise to keep to the other path, well clear of the edge.)

Looking down one of the gullies above Wastwater

This glory extends for about one mile, as far as the top of Illgill Head, after which things are a little more sober as the path drops down duller grass slopes to the gap between Illgill Head and Sca Fell – although even Sca Fell looks a bit coy from this angle, taking on the appearance of yet another large, rounded lump of a thing.

To the right lies Burnmoor Tarn. This isn't on the route, but it is notable for the extended dour landscape in which it lies, in sharp contrast to the fells around Wastwater. There is a house on its southern edge, not at all pretty – semi-derelict even – that adds to the dark feel of the place. It looks like the kind of house hapless American teenagers would insist on spending the night in, despite the rising storm and the warnings of the crazy drooling local, in a down-market Hollywood thriller. Burnmoor Lodge was built in the 19th century, far from any roads, so it must have taken a considerable effort on someone's part. It seems odd to have invested so much in a location that is, to put it mildly, not the most attractive of all the options that were available to choose from.

The route lies to the left, following a path down almost as far as Brackenclose, before doubling back along the lake shore.

At first this path is an easy stroll, with a pleasant view over the lake, and the steeply angled slopes of Illgill Head above. In fact more than half of the lakeside path is pretty easy going. But eventually the screes are reached, and things become more demanding. Nothing too hard at first – just watch your footing – but soon the boulders get bigger and bigger, until they're larger than you, while any pretence of a visible path disappears completely; suddenly you're on your own, having to improvise a way over huge, steeply piled boulders, often non-too stable, sometimes blocking your path in walls, sometimes opening into trenches that must be climbed down. Mental pictures of snapped shins and broken ankles have to be suppressed as your boots slip into gaps or the rocks suddenly tilt.

Walking on the Wastwater Screes

For many of us this is, of course, great fun, and eventually, possibly with some relief, you reach the edge of the boulders and enter a wooded area. From here the walk is easy once again, genuinely pleasant among the hawthorns that stubbornly draw a living out of the poor rocky soil, and you will soon reach the foot of the lake where the day began, passing the pumping station at the head of the River Irt – once recommended by Wainwright as somewhere to dry your socks over the building's warm air outlet.

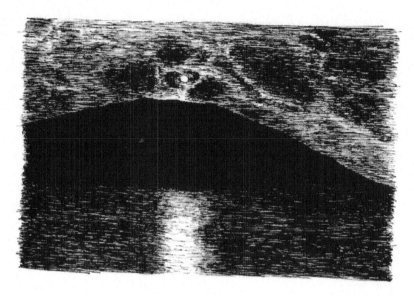

The moon rising over Illgill Head

Scafell Pike and Sca Fell

Scafell Pike, on the left, and Sca Fell, on the right

As everyone knows, Scafell Pike is the highest mountain in England, at 3,209 feet or 978 metres. It is also one of the least hospitable. Its summit is a great rounded hump strewn with boulders that must be slogged over to reach the trig point and the stone shelter nearby; there are no paths in the normal sense, just lines of marker cairns and scratches on the rocks to show where others have gone before you. Because the top is a broad dome there's no heightened sense of achievement when you reach the shelter, as there is on other fells with more obvious or dramatic summits – just relief that you've got there at last. Even in summer it can be a bleak place, with snow and ice lasting until late in the year, while it's regularly enveloped in mist, so the views – which, it must be granted are extensive and spectacular – may not even be visible. As if all this was not enough, England's highest mountain suffers the almost daily humiliation of being tramped over at speed by Three-Peakers, only interested in getting up and down again as quickly as possible.

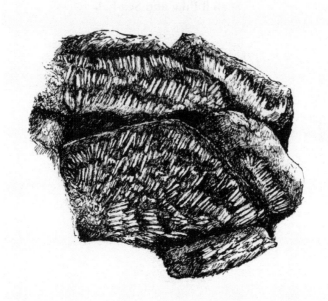

Rime ice on the stones of the shelter on the top of Scafell Pike. This was in May, and there was still much ice and snow on the ground.

However, the Pike is surrounded by splendid things, and some of its ascents are both magnificent and tough physical challenges. On clear days the catalogue of mountains and fell tops that can be seen is extensive: Broad Crag, Ill Crag, Great End, Great Gable, Bowfell and many more all lie in the immediate vicinity, while in good weather, to the north, you can see as far as Skiddaw and Blencathra; the peaks of the Mosedale horseshoe lie to the north-west, and, perhaps most dramatic of all, the Pike's great partner, Sca Fell, is only a few hundred yards away as the crow flies to the south-west.

This naming is confusing for beginners. Scafell Pike, being the highest, has the longer name, but, it has to be said, is the least interesting of the two; Sca Fell isn't quite as high at 3,163 feet (964 metres), so deserves its shorter name, but is by far the more dramatic peak because, unlike the Pike, its summit is guarded by a steep wall of crags and rocks whose curving humped profile is easily recognisable from viewpoints all over the Lake District, making it a hard-won objective if tackled from the northern side. The two classic walker's routes through these defences are via Lord's Rake, which entails an exciting but difficult clamber up a rock gully, and Foxes Tarn, a route that is easier than the rake but made unpleasant by path erosion and a consequent sliding mass of scree and rubble. (The tarn is tiny – one of the smallest in the area to have a name.) Easier but less exciting routes are available via the fell's long southern flank that extends down to Eskdale, or up its western flank, from Wastwater or Burnmoor Tarn.

The two peaks, Scafell Pike and Sca Fell, are linked by Mickledore, one of those famed places in the Lake District; a sharp-edged ridge connecting two grand old mountains. It's a long, inverted V, with a smooth face on the south-east side and a steep, stony face on the north-west, the start of the long descent to Wasdale. A stretcher box tucked into the shelter of the rocks reminds you that this can be a dangerous place, especially in bad weather, which is not exactly an unusual occurrence up here. In heavy mist it can be very eerie. One moment you may be in sight of other walkers all around, then fifteen minutes later, once the silent white blankness descends, it seems they have all vanished, safely returned to their hotels and B&Bs, while you are left all alone on the mountain. Your sense of distance and perspective becomes completely distorted, so what were clear paths become sketchy and fizzle out; rock walls loom up unexpectedly; precipitous drops open at your feet without warning; the stretcher box appears in the wrong place, moved by the gremlins of the mists. It's at times like this that you thank the people who went to the trouble of constructing those lines of cairns that are cleverly spaced so that, just as you reach one, the next becomes visible as a murky silhouette in the cold white mists ahead.

But in clear weather, which does happen, the view across Mickledore to Scafell is quite special, for it looks right over to the rocky defences of the fell, to the great craggy wall known as Broad Stand.

Broad Stand

Mickledore and Broad Stand

There are many stories about this place. This is where, many years ago, Coleridge got stuck and nearly lost his life. He had climbed Sca Fell from Brackenclose in Wasdale, and was attempting to cross over Mickledore to Scafell Pike. His route-finding methods were not very sophisticated, as he later explained in a letter to his great love, Sara Hutchinson.

'There is a sort of gambling, to which I am much addicted,' he began. 'It is this. When I find it convenient to descend a mountain, I am too confident and too indolent to look round about and wind about 'till I find a track or other symptom of safety; but I wander on, and where it is first possible to descend, there I go – relying on fortune for how far down this possibility will continue.'

So he took a direct line-of-sight route, straight over the edge of Broad Stand. The fortune he was relying on did not stay with him for long. About halfway down he came to 'a smooth perpendicular rock about seven feet high – this was nothing. I put my hands on the ledge and dropped down.' This was nothing? Sara must have been thrilled! He carried on dropping down in

148

this way, but the exertion and tension 'put my limbs in a tremble' and he began to have doubts about continuing. Unfortunately it was not possible to get back up, while 'every drop increased the palsy of my limbs, I shook all over,' but not, he assured Sara, out of fear.

He came to the point where he had two more drops to make: 'The first of these two was tremendous. It was twice my own height, and the ledge at the bottom was so exceedingly narrow, that if I dropt down upon it I must of necessity have fallen backwards and of course killed myself.' At this point most people would, I think, be starting to wrestle with rising panic. No way up, no way down, trembling limbs, and sudden death all too close. So what did he do? He lay down on his back and laughed at himself 'for a madman'. He 'lay in a state of almost prophetic trance and delight, and blessed God aloud'.

This self-administered therapy must have helped, for after a while he recovered enough to carry on. He came across a stinking dead sheep that had fallen to its death and which did little for his nervous state of mind, but then he found a vertical split in the rock. 'I measured the breadth of the rent, and found that there was no danger of my being wedged in, so I put my knapsack round to my side and slipped down as between two walls, without any danger or difficulty.' Presumably he had chanced upon the climber's route now known as 'fat man's agony'.

He did, of course, get to the bottom without mishap, but found that his whole breast was covered in 'great red heat bumps, so thick that no hair could lie between them.' They were still with him the next day as he wrote to Sara, vivid physical evidence of the stress he had been under.

So, as Coleridge no doubt admitted later in the pub, Broad Stand is not a walker's route, up or down. In fact it is dangerous, and there are accidents there every year, some of them fatal. Sitting on the flanks of Scafell Pike munching sandwiches one sunny day, I watched as people swarmed over Sca Fell and Broad Stand looking for ways down – none of them, presumably, having read their Coleridge. 'Just do it' seemed to be their motto, adopted at the time they bought their trainers. Later, after descending, as I passed the car park at Brackenclose, the mountain rescue team arrived, jumped out of their Landrover and *ran* up the slopes I had just come down, as a rescue helicopter circled overhead.

Lord's Rake

Many years ago, while walking in the Scafell range, one of our group said he knew an interesting route up Sca Fell. He had no map or guide book, but someone had shown him the way once before. Always ready for a challenge, I agreed to try it with him and we set off together. From Mickledore, he led the way along a narrow path that crept below the vertical crags of Sca Fell until eventually we came to a gaping crevice, a rocky gully rising straight up on our left-hand side. That was our route, and he led us up the steep passageway – an ascent that I remember being quite hard going because of its steepness and that the ground was very loose under foot. Towards the top there was an especially awkward section where you had to climb up the right-hand wall, with the rock crumbling away beneath hands and boots. But we got to the top without undue fuss, and with a buzz of achievement.

Later I read in St Alf's book *The Southern Fells* that this gully was Lord's Rake, and that it was, in fact, a notoriously difficult scramble. The result was that the next time I went there, knowing it was difficult, it turned out that it was indeed difficult – much more so than the first time. This, I suppose, is an example of the corrupting effect of guidebooks.

Lord's Rake, filled with snow

Wainwright also said that Lord's Rake is safe. I wonder. Even in good weather one can feel quite uneasy, struggling up the sliding rubble in the gully or the crumbling rock faces on either side. Once, on a later expedition, as a group of us approached the Rake from Hollow Stones, we were met by someone coming the opposite way with blood running down his head. He had been hit by a falling stone, was very upset, and strongly advised us not to go near the place.

The real difficulty with Lord's Rake is the combination of its steepness and the loose scree that fills the gully. For long stretches there is no secure grip or foothold, and the task is to maintain enough forward momentum to offset the slow backsliding undertow of the scree beneath your feet.

But now there is an additional twist: in 2002 a large rock slab broke away from the side of the Rake and came to rest leaning up against the left-hand wall, right at the top of the gully. Warning signs were put up advising people not to use the rake at all, because the slab was precariously balanced and might become dislodged at any time. And it certainly looks precarious; a huge weight of rock held in place only by its very tip, wedged up against the side of the gully. Yet over ten years later the slab is still there, the sign has gone, and people are climbing the Rake once more. One day that rock will dislodge itself and fall, and the fall will be spectacular, but whether it will happen next week, next year or in a century's time, no one can say.

Pulpit Rock: a great feathered flight of rock thrusting diagonally into the air. This is the view as seen from the ascent from Hollow Stones to Mickledore, just below Lord's Rake.

Piers Gill

This is an excellent route up to Scafell Pike, one that seems to be less used than many others. Piers Gill is a deep ravine cutting into the slopes of Lingmell, with a sharp left-hand bend that twists to point directly along the route to the summit. From Wasdale Head it is reached by following the heavily used path along the north side of Lingmell Beck, passing between the overhanging crags of Lingmell on one side and Great Gable on the other. There is a pretty double waterfall and pool where two streams meet, the deep water often as blue as the sky, just after which you cross over and fork to the right.

The Gill reveals itself to you at this point, and you'll be able to look directly into and along the length of its deep chasm leading up to Lingmell. It may be tempting to try to follow the stream at its bottom, but all advice is against, for the Gill is impassable further up, while its steep sides cannot be scaled. Piers Gill has its dark side, a history of fatal accidents.

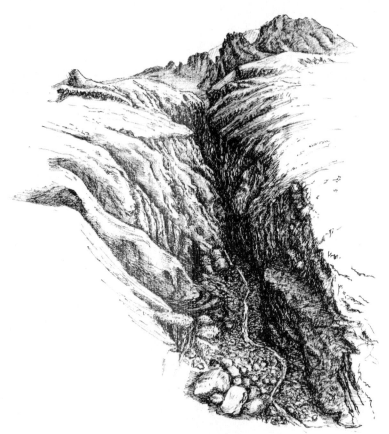

Peering into Piers Gill

The path keeps to the left or east side of the Gill, staying quite close to the edge. It is worth exploring a little to see the spectacular view into the ravine, but all the usual warnings about taking care apply because the edge is eroded and crumbling in places. The path is relatively easy walking except at one point where it ascends a steep stretch of rock, requiring some scrambling. As so often, this is more of a challenge in descent than ascent, but there are plenty of hand and footholds.

Further up, just before the sharp bend to the left, there are paths that try to seduce you away from the edge into the area called Middleboot Knots, but it's worth continuing with the ravine edge until it eventually peters out. The way continues straight on in a south-easterly direction into the gap before you between Broad Crag on the left and Scafell Pike on the right. The scenery is now rough and stony, and it has to be said the last couple of hundred feet of ascent to the top of the Pike is not greatly enjoyable because of the steepness and the wastes of loose rubble you must cross. However, almost as soon as the path levels off, the summit cairn and trig point can be seen.

Wasdale Head and rock climbing

Wasdale Head – the first syllable pronounced as in the word 'was' and not, as I thought for so long, as in 'vast' – is perhaps the grandest location in the whole Lake District for the walker. Difficult to get to (compared to other valleys), surrounded by great mountains and fells, and with England's deepest lake and its screes nearby, all these things make it irresistible. There are comforts too, but not many; just sufficient to sustain you over a few days' energetic but rewarding walking and, for some, climbing.

Wasdale Head is where rock climbing began in England, back in the late nineteenth century. It was largely the sport of the wealthier, leisured classes: young men from privileged backgrounds, hungry for adventure. They would gather in the bars of the Wasdale Head Inn to swap stories and plan daring new climbs, amusing themselves by playing games like the Billiard Room Traverse, which involved doing a circuit of the room with their hands gripping the edge of the table and their feet walking around the wall, close to the ceiling. Names like Walter Parry Haskett-Smith and Owen Glynne Jones are still remembered among the climbing community because of their exploits, making the first ascent of so many crags, slabs and gullies. Sometimes they were accompanied by the Abraham brothers, photographers from Keswick who would climb up the mountains loaded with heavy wooden cameras so they could record the adventurers' exploits, requiring them to hold their perilous poses for the long exposure times the technology of the day required. Many of their photographs appeared in Owen Glynne Jones' book *Rock-climbing in the English Lake District*, first published in 1897.

And there they still are, up on the walls of the Inn, all those young men nonchalantly hanging off rock faces or standing casually on the top of Napes Needle, looking faintly bored and in possession of no more specialist equipment than a tweed jacket and a pipe. Sometimes they have ropes, but carried in a way that suggests they are more for the camera than practical use. They are the epitome of cool, long before anyone knew the modern meaning of the word. Look closely and there is something even more startling: a view of Napes Needle with a woman climber standing on the top. The surprise isn't so much that it's a woman, but that she is wearing a fashionable hat and full-length Victorian skirts[16].

---

[16] Owen Glynne Jones wrote: 'One photograph exists of the Needle in which

The locals, of course, thought they were mad. Maybe they were. I look at these old photographs and some visceral response in me says 'No, don't go there'. Being no climber, I feel pretty much the same when looking at modern photographs of rock climbers in action, or when standing in the shadow of a famous climb like Scafell's Central Buttress. It's an involuntary survival instinct. But while modern climbers are unquestionably engaged in a dangerous sport requiring skill and ice-cool nerves, they also draw on the experience of all those who have gone before them. My copy of *100 Classic Climbs*, bought to browse with my feet safely on horizontal ground, has each climb described in meticulous detail and illustrated with schematic diagrams, so while there is always danger, there need be no uncertainty about whether a chosen route is feasible or an impossibility leading to a sudden death. Those early explorers had no such advantage.

In the early 1880s, Walter Parry Haskett-Smith caught a momentary glimpse of a rock pillar high up on Great Gable, unveiled briefly as the cloud swirled about. In 1884 he returned with a companion, and set about finding it again. They succeeded, but made no attempt to climb it. Two years later he returned and, setting out alone one afternoon, decided to go back to this mysterious pillar. It seems that on the way he went up Central Gully on Gable Crag – the first ascent ever made thereof – and then came down Needle Ridge, which he later described as 'quite feasible'. This brought him to the Needle which, almost on impulse, he climbed, on his own. Just in case no one believed his story later, he left his handkerchief on the top, held down by a stone.

The scale of his achievement is hard to overstate. Napes Needle is a pillar of rock some twenty metres high, narrowing to a pointed wedge at the top. Its sides are close to vertical and there's a large overhang on one face, just below the top. There are deep cracks in the sides that Haskett-Smith made use of, but they only got him so far, and when he paused to consider how to conquer the last two blocks his chief concern was whether the top, which he could not see, would be flat, with edges that he could grip and haul himself up by, or smoothly rounded, offering no sanctuary. His method was to toss flat stones up and see if they stayed on the top or slid off: one out of three stayed put, and that was good enough for him. He reached the top shortly after.

These days you can watch people on YouTube climbing the Needle as if it were nothing at all. Which, I realise, is the same impression those climbers of long ago liked to give. But what is obvious enough just looking at the Needle is that coming down is even harder. In his account of the descent,

---

nearly all the climbing details are masked by a crowd of daring maidens swarming up it.' Now that would be worth seeing, but I never have.

Haskett-Smith merely says there was an 'anxious moment, but the rest went easily enough'. Standing on firm ground once more he noted his satisfaction at seeing his handkerchief fluttering in the breeze high above.

That climb became famous, and it wasn't long before many others made the same ascent, including those extraordinary women in long skirts. The previously unassailable craggy faces of Great Gable, Pillar and Scafell were all explored and conquered, as were rock faces in all the other valleys and fellsides in Lakeland; rock climbing was established as a sport in England.

The cool bravery that drove the early pioneers also accompanied many of them to the First World War trenches from which not all returned. There is a war memorial to them on the top of Great Gable, erected in 1924 by the Rock and Fell Climbing Club, which had held its first meeting in the Wasdale Head Inn. Owen Glynne Jones, brave to the point of recklessness, was to die in a climbing accident in Switzerland at the age of 32. Walter Parry Haskett-Smith was luckier, living into his late 80s. Fifty years after his lone ascent of the Needle, he repeated the feat, this time with ropes and companions; he was 76 years old at the time, so could be excused for having gone a bit soft.

I look on the activities of rock climbers as an outsider. Slightly in awe of them, my main feeling when seeing them in action is similar to those Wasdale farmers over a century ago: they are crazy. But they have a degree of wit. Here, for example, is the grading system, actually one of several, used to classify climbs. It starts simply enough:

Easy
Moderate
Difficult

Then it goes up a gear:

> Hard difficult
> Very difficult
> Hard very difficult

Having exhausted those permutations, we have 'severe', which comes in several variants:

> Mild severe
> Severe
> Hard severe
> Mild very severe
> Very severe

'Very severe' sounds bad enough, but there is more:

> Very severe (hard)
> Hard very severe
> Mild extremely severe
> Extremely severe

That seems to cover all the possibilities. Elsewhere in this book I describe the difficulties I had climbing Easy Gully, on Pavey Ark. My guess is that Easy Gully was given its name by climbers, and it does my self-esteem no great good to see that 'Easy' is the lowest grade on a scale of fifteen.

Then there are the names. Fellwalkers know their fells by names that are well established, with roots that go back many generations – or so we imagine. But rock climbers were exploring new territory and, like Adam in the Garden of Eden, they needed to give names to things not named before. Unlike Adam they had no divine guidance, and their method, if there was one, was very modern indeed. Here are a few taken from *100 Classic Climbs*.

> 'The Mysteron', on Buckbarrow, in Wasdale
> 'Megaton', on Pillar, Ennerdale
> 'The Mortician', Black Crag, Borrowdale
> 'DDT', on Goat Crag, Borrowdale, situated right next to 'Praying Mantis'
> 'Where Eagles Squawk', Eagle Crag, Borrowdale
> 'Communist Convert', on Raven Crag at the north end of Thirlmere, no doubt converted by the nearby 'Totalitarian'
> 'Laugh Not', on White Ghyll, Langdale, where its friends are 'Slip Knot', 'Gordian Knot' and 'Haste Not'
> 'Gandalf's Groove' – inevitably there had to be at least one reference to

Tolkeiny nonsense – on Neckband Crag, Langdale
'Sword of Damocles', on North Buttress, Langdale
'Gormenghast', on Heron Crag, Eskdale

And, finally:

'Samba Pa Ti', on Dow Crag, presumably named by a fan of Carlos Santana, who made an album with that name but has so far failed to return the compliment by releasing another called 'Goat's Water'.

Great Gable

Great Gable may be one of the most famous mountains in the Lake District, not just for its splendid name but because of its majestic appearance, obvious to anyone visiting Wastwater, whether or not they are walkers. There it stands, mounting guard at the far end of the valley, triangular in profile and topped by crags that look somehow as if the mountain has its head tilted downwards to peer at its feet in the valley, far below.

Great Gable, viewed from Wasdale Head

Great Gable earned its name well, being a serious mountain demanding serious minds and serious work from its would-be conquerors, so while the route described here may be one of the easiest ascents, in this context the term 'easy' is relative. It begins at Burnthwaite Farm at the head of Wasdale, where there is a clear path veering right along what is known as Moses Trod, following Lingmell Beck into the deep valley between Lingmell and Great Gable. Before long you reach the foot of the long grassy arête down the angular edge of the Gable; a path offers a direct way up, but for now we merely keep it in mind for later in the day, when it will provide our descent.

A little further on and the path divides again. The lower route follows the valley bottom for a couple of kilometres until it rises sharply at the head, with a steep climb up to Sty Head. The higher path, on the left, climbs diagonally across the face of Great Gable at a steady gradient until it too reaches Sty Head. You can take your pick. The higher path is now built up to the point that it's possible to find yourself on it having completely missed the division of paths. Flat and broad, with an easy gradient, it is by far the most commonly used route, especially by those in a hurry. Wainwright was quite disparaging about this, declaring that time was to be spent, not saved. Maybe he had a point, but there is plenty of interest to see from this path, with the Gable's towering crags high above on the left, the valley floor falling away to the right, Lingmell's jagged edge rising above the opposite side and, before long, a spectacular view of Piers Gill, that deep chasm cut into the mountain side, with its distinctive right-angled bend that points directly up towards the scree-filled gully between Broad Crag and Scafell Pike.

It is only towards the very top that this path ceases to be something of a bridleway, and for a few metres hands may be needed to steady your way up some rough but safe rocks. And then, there you are, at Sty Head, with dizzying views back down the valley and across to Great End and the sweeping curve of mountains at the valley head. After pausing here, a few paces further will take you to the stretcher box, with Sty Head Tarn directly in front.

Styhead Tarn merits a mention of its own, not because it is pretty (it isn't, being rather sombre – a little dull, even) but because it lies close to one of the busiest crossing points in the mountains. In the summer, hundreds, maybe thousands of people march past it every day, hurrying to or from Great Gable, Great End, Scafell Pike and the rest of the Scafell range. There's a stretcher box on the path, near the tarn, with the slopes of Great Gable behind it, and beyond that the yawning space that is the upper end of Wasdale. Lingmell is opposite, with its steeply falling crags terminating a great curving procession of fells from Great End, to Broad Crag and Scafell Pike. To the left the Corridor Route can be seen snaking its way over the fellsides to the great Pike, while directly opposite is possibly the best high-level view of Piers Gill that there is.

A view of Piers Gill, a great chasm in the fellside, seen from Sty Head

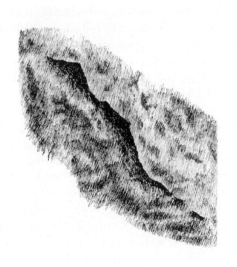

Sometimes the views aren't viewable. This is the edge of Lingmell emerging from the mist.

There is a route straight up the Gable from the stretcher box, although it's very rough, being much tramped. Instead, we follow the path down to the tarn, passing along its left-hand bank, all the while looking for the second path up, to the left. For such a well-used route it's surprising that it is not especially obvious. There is no trampled crossing of ways, as in so many other places, like in front of the stretcher box just passed, where the ground is criss-crossed with paths to the point of confusion. However, there is a turn-off just beyond the tarn that leads directly up the depression between Great Gable and its adjacent little brother, Green Gable. This is Aaron Slack, and if the path is hard to find, simply make a beeline for the gully between the two mountains; the path soon appears, for it is built up and easy to follow, starting on the left-hand side of the stream that runs off the mountains and later crossing to the right. After a while the stream disappears from view, going subterranean, but you can still hear the water gurgling away beneath the stones you're walking on.

Things start well, but eventually the built-up path disappears, overwhelmed by the profusion of rubble churned up by boots and rain and cascading water. Progress now is slower over great masses of sliding, unstable small stones, piled at a steep gradient in the gully between the two mountains. It is safe but exhausting, each step countered by the constant backsliding of the stones underfoot, a wearying drag on your progress. Once, while making this ascent in torrential rain, I met a cyclist coming down, his knees streaming with blood, and his bike, a useless encumbrance, heaved up onto his shoulder. He seemed cheerful enough, calling out hello as we passed and apparently happy, if lacking in judgement.

In time and with some relief you arrive at Windy Gap, the saddle between Great and Green Gables, named for reasons that will be obvious enough. After a pause to catch your breath, it's time for the final stage.

From Windy Gap the ascent is rocky, and quite tricky in the wet. There's a confusion of paths and cairns, the result of many people swarming up here over the years. As I scrambled up one time in mist it struck me that if I was on my own, which I was, and there was no sign of other people having been there before me, then I would have probably begun to think myself a little crazy, for the climb is rough, and the mist makes it impossible to see ahead or judge the safety or otherwise of your chosen direction. It's the messy evidence of people who passed this way before that brings confidence.

At the top there is a war memorial, a panel set into the rock by the Fell and Rock Climbing Club in 1924 to commemorate members of the club who died in the 1914–18 war. Above the list of names there is a three-dimensional map of Great Gable and the surrounding fells, cast in bronze. As I peered at this sombre record I noticed something on the ground at the base of the monument: a small pile of greyish gritty powder. In the grounds of St Olaf's church, back at Wasdale Head, there are notices asking please, do not scatter cremation ashes in the grounds of the church. Presumably it's unsightly, not to say a tiny bit selfish. But St Olaf's authority does not extend this far, and its prohibition stays down in the valley.

With visibility little more than a few yards, I took a compass bearing to find a route off, opting for the path leading north-west, along a line of cairns laid out so that just as you reach one, the next appears out of the mist to lead you on. The descent, which is marked on the OS map, follows the north-west edge of the mountain, and is horrible. Steep, rocky, crumbling, criss-crossed with contradictory lines of cairns and paths that lead nowhere, it is the mirror image of the route up, but this time rational reflection did not lead me to any reconciliation. It's a depressing ruin of a path. There was some respite as I dropped below the mist and the view over Ennerdale and Haystacks opened up, but this is not a descent that offers any pleasure, and it was relentless right down to Beck Head, at the foot of Great Gable's screes.

Ah yes, the screes. On a descent even further back in the past I did, I confess, run down the screes. Deplorable of course, but also great fun, fast and thrilling. I was down in no time at all. Obviously, I am not advocating this now, for today scree-running is very bad indeed – something we must not do – but it certainly beat that north-west descent hands down, and so far as I can see there's still plenty of scree on the flanks of Great Gable.

The direction is now more or less due south, beneath those screes. If the cloud has lifted, a magnificent view straight over Wastwater out to the sea opens up, framed by the crags of Lingmell and Yewbarrow. On a clear evening the setting sun will be in your face, low over the sea, casting long shadows and painting the Wastwater screes gold and pink.

The view over Wastwater from Great Gable

This path is part of the Gable Girdle – a route that encircles the mountain, passing below the Great Napes, those stooping crags seen earlier from Wasdale, with Napes Needle tucked away among them. When the south-west arête is reached, we leave the girdle path and march straight down the edge, where, after a little way, a remarkable thing happens. The path, for so long a hard grind over rough and broken ground, is suddenly rich green turf, springy underfoot and hardly marked by boots. How can this be, on such a heavily used path? It's a mystery, but a welcome one, providing a comfortable way back down to where we began, and the track to Burnthwaite Farm.

Napes Needle

That isn't the possessive term: there is no Mr Nape. The Napes are the tilted, wild-looking crags near the top of Great Gable, hanging over Wasdale and giving the mountain that appearance of bending forward to look down at its own foot. The Needle stands out from them, hard to see from ground level but visible when you know what to look for, especially when the sun is shining low up Wasdale. It appears, not as it is famously portrayed in drawings and photographs, but as a gleaming white rectangle high up on the crags above a narrow scree run, the shining face of the angular rock pyramid that caps the needle.

Napes Needle is strictly for climbers, but it is possible to get to its base without too much trouble. The south traverse is a path across the southern face of Great Gable from the Wasdale arête to Styhead that passes right under the crags; it is part of the Gable Girdle, which passes all the way round Great Gable at heights varying between 1,500 and 2,500 feet (460 and 760 metres). On the west side it passes over the flanks of the mountain just above the small tarns at Beck Head. A large cairn marks the place where several paths meet, but the traverse path isn't among them and it's not so easy to identify. It lies a little higher up the boulder field that covers this side of the mountain; a small cairn marks it, but takes some looking for.

From the little cairn the path is clear. It's not so much a path as a trail of brown marks on the chaotically strewn rocks where walkers' boots have polished off the surface layers of lichen. Although you're moving along a steady contour, neither rising nor falling to any degree, the mountain side is steep, and it's wise to maintain respectful attention to your situation.

Once past the arête above Wasdale the nature of the path changes; the scree is left behind to be replaced by an easy but enjoyable scramble along the solid rock that skirts the lower edge of the Napes. Progress is interrupted by Little Hell Gate – a reddish scree run that must be crossed with a degree of boldness – which is followed by another stretch on firm rock and then a second, narrower, scree run. Neither of these runs is quite as alarming as might be imagined, not in good weather at any rate. If you look up from the midst of the second run you should be able to make out the Needle high up on the right-hand side of the gully, remembering that from this angle it does not look like you would expect from the classic photographs.

The Cat Rock, sometimes called The Sphinx. This can be seen from the narrow scree run that leads up to the Needle.

Judging by the scuffed state of the scree, many people go straight up to the Needle from here, but less damage is done by continuing along the traverse path for a few tens of yards until, just before an even bigger scree run, ominously named Great Hell Gate, a path doubles back to the left, up the slope. It leads back to the narrower run, but having gained some useful height. From this point there is no avoiding the scree, but a few minutes of determined work will get you to the top. When I went I was concentrating so hard on the scrambling that I didn't look up until I'd got to the top of the gully, and was startled to see this.

Napes Needle, viewed from its base

This still isn't quite the classic view; to see that you have to get to the Dress Circle, higher up the rocks on the left-hand side of the gully, but this was as far as I felt willing or able to go on my own. The power of the Needle isn't just its height – although that certainly counts – but the bizarre juxtaposition of its slender lower shank and that great wedge of rock on the top with its dramatic overhang. It surely shouldn't exist at all, it seems so improbable, but there it is: solid, real, undeniable.

Great Gable as a landmark

Great Gable's huge bulk is visible from all across the Lake District, making it a useful landmark, but its shape varies depending on which angle you view it from. Its southern aspect is dominated by the nodding Napes, while from the north it can be seen from miles off as a huge rounded dome with a dark foreboding face. From the east and west it has a rectangular profile, and can be seen from the far eastern fells as a sort of blister on the horizon. From the west it looks like an enormous fruitcake.

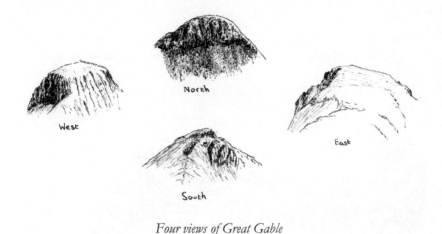

Four views of Great Gable

Great End and Cust's Gully

Cust's Gully is high up on the face of Great End, a thrilling cleft in the rockface with vertical sides supporting a huge chock stone jammed between them high overhead. You can see it from the path between Styhead and Sprinkling Tarns as you pass over the rise that drops down to Sprinkling Tarn. It's on the right-hand end of Great End's rocky face; binoculars will confirm it, if there's any doubt.

Great End seen from Sprinkling Tarn: a dark, brooding wall of crags that gets so little sun that patches of ice and snow remain on it until well into the spring

Sprinkling Tarn, seen from Great End

Wainwright described his two failed attempts to climb the gully and he concluded this was 'no way for walkers'. On reading his account three decades ago with friends, we decided to go and have a look. We made our way round to the gully and after making a rather desultory exploration, decided that he was right: there was no way through. I suspect that having read Wainwright's warnings this was something of a forgone conclusion.

Remembering this long afterwards, I thought it would be good to go and get a few drawings. This came up in conversation over breakfast in the hostel where I was staying.

'Where are you going today?' a fellow hosteller asked, the standard opening line over the greasy fry-up. He was quiet spoken, with a Yorkshire accent.

'I thought I'd take a look at Cust's Gully.'

He looked up, suddenly interested. 'Cust's Gully?' he said, with unexpected emphasis. 'Have you read Wainwright's account of it?'

'Well, yes. But I only want to look at it, not climb it. Do you know it?'

It turned out he had climbed Cust's a couple of years before. 'The thing is, Wainwright said there was one difficult pitch, the one that defeated him, but after that it was an easy scramble to the top. But of course he'd never actually climbed it. I went up there and got past the first pitch, only to find there was a second one, even harder. I felt somewhat aggrieved at that.'

Evidently enough he'd got up without mishap ('I told myself I wouldn't fall more than ten to twelve feet') but had no intention of ever trying again.

He looked doubtful: 'It's a hard climb just getting up to it, you know.'

Oh dear, he's thinking: what's this old duffer getting up to?

He was right about the climb. From the path to Sprinkling Tarn, just beyond where the gully first comes into view, it's clear what you're aiming for, but less clear how to get there. At first it's easy, over rough grass and heather, but it's not long until the gradient becomes steep, and it's a matter of clutching at grass and rocks to haul yourself up. There is no path, only short stretches of what might one day become paths, betrayed by patches of trampled rubble and discarded Mars Bar wrappers, but mostly you're on your own. It was very wet that day, and everything was slippery – the grass, the moss, the slimy lichen-covered rocks – and the mist was already rolling in from the west. Worrisome thoughts broke in: suppose I get stuck, or the mist closes in and I get lost? This was no place to be with no path and no visibility. Romantic ideas about lounging at the bottom of the Gully, pencil in one hand and sketch pad in the other, were forgotten; once I got there, out came the camera, snap, snap, snap, and away I went down again. By the time I got to the tarn, the heights of Great End were lost in white clouds.

Cust's Gully rises very steeply between impressively smooth rock walls. Even at the entrance the ground is so steep and rough that it takes concentration to maintain balance. The chockstone hanging high above makes the whole thing doubly impressive. It looks secure enough, but the stones piled on top of it may be less so. The gully is named after Arthur Cust, who made the first recorded ascent in 1880.

Yewbarrow to Mosedale

There are two classic views of Wastwater, repeated over and over in photographs and paintings. One is of the screes, while the other is the view over the length of the lake towards three great fells which, from this position, take on giant triangular profiles. Great Gable is in the middle, flanked by Lingmell to its right, while on the left, standing well forward of the others, is Yewbarrow.

Yewbarrow from the lakeside

Yewbarrow is long and narrow, almost perfectly triangular in cross-section, and with its long curved spine, from some angles it resembles a prehistoric exhibit from the Natural History Museum. Although from the far end of the lake it might look like it's connected to Great Gable, it is not, for the north end of Yewbarrow is one side of the gateway to the Mosedale valley, and the start – or end – of a tremendous horse-shoe ridge walk above that valley, taking in Red Pike, Scoat Fell and Pillar.

The ascent from the lakeside starts at a car park at Overbeck Bridge. It doesn't waste any time, launching almost immediately into a lung-bursting climb straight up the ridge of the mountain towards the crags hanging above. Climbing it recently I realised I had not been that way for many years, when the section through the crags was unnervingly difficult because of its eroded state. Fortunately this is no longer so. Much work has been done on this section of the path up to and through the 'Great Door'. It seems to have been partially re-routed to avoid the old damaged areas, and a new path built, carefully angled and stepped. There is only one slightly tricky section above a short stretch of old stone wall built long ago to stop sheep falling down the gully, where the rocky surface made it impossible to build a path. Otherwise it's an enjoyable scramble up to the long backbone of the fell, from where the walking is easy and the views excellent.

The north end of Yewbarrow mirrors the south with a steep drop over

Stirrup Crag. This is quite a tough, rocky little job, requiring careful use of fingers, toes and backside; throw your walking poles down to the bottom and follow them. Below the firm rocky section the path degenerates somewhat; no repairs have been done here, and the area is criss-crossed with tracks people have created this way and that, all the way down to Dore Head at the bottom. Now turn back and look at what you've just descended: you might be surprised.

Stirrup Crag, at the northern end of Yewbarrow

From here, Red Pike calls for attention. This is one of those mountains that has two personalities. Its western side is all long, slow, undulating curves rising up to a ridge that peaks like a breaking wave hanging over its eastern side, a precipitous mass of crags and gullies steeply tumbling all the way down to Mosedale bottom. Red Pike is the highest point of this wave.

The path tends to stay away from the edge, and unless you take care to track your position you might find that you've skirted Red Pike without visiting its highest point, and have to back-track. The view down into Mosedale is something almost to be meditated on. It is another huge glacial valley, with the elegantly sculptured profile such valleys have, and it conveys a sense of vast space, lonely and somewhat melancholy – profound even – with the occasional distant bleat of a sheep only adding to the feeling.

Unfortunately meditation and westerly gales do not mix well, and so we must press on, continuing along the western side of the ridge towards Scoat Fell, the summit of which could be in any number of places. From there the direction of travel is obvious in a strategic sense – look for Pillar and head for it via Wind Gap – but the detail is much less certain, because the 'path' disappears among a jumble of huge boulders.

The chaotic path on Scoat Fell

Steeple can also be seen to the north of Scoat Fell, connected to it by a ridge. Here is another mountain with an unmistakable profile: a pointed tower of rocky cliffs.

Steeple

There is a scree path at Wind Gap that offers a quick way off the ridge down to Mosedale. The sun was getting low when I got this far, and so I took this option. It was horrible.

One is not surprised to find that it is very steep; even a cursory glance at a map makes that clear. Nor that, being full of scree, it is rough. But the rocks are large and treacherous – there is no question of scree running – making progress laboriously slow and tiring. Indeed by the time I reached the bottom I wondered how much time I really had saved, compared to continuing over Pillar and down Black Sail Pass. Once past the scree the path is easier, much of it on grass and almost free of erosion; with the practical knowledge just acquired it did not seem so surprising to find that not many people come this way. Still, the walk through Mosedale was pleasant, and there was time to reflect on the day's experience over a beer and a dinner in Ritson's Bar at the Wasdale Head Inn.

10 CONISTON

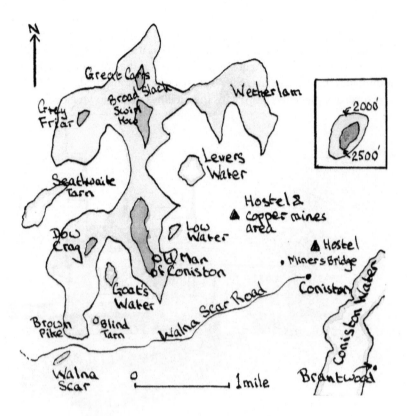

Coniston relies on tourism for its livelihood as much as anywhere in the Lakes, but it has the air of a busy, lived-in place, large enough to have its own fire station, library, primary and secondary schools, museum, post office, ancient hall, two youth hostels, a working quarry and a brewery. It has a long industrial history, based on mining for slate and copper, and at least two famous adopted sons – John Ruskin and Donald Campbell – both of them remembered in the museum, and one of them, Ruskin, buried in the churchyard.

The town is set back from the lake a little, and there's a pleasant walk down to the lakeside and its shingle beach where families idle away summer afternoons, and a jetty from where you can take a ferry tour around or across the lake.

A little way along the shore is Coniston Hall, a building dating back to the 16th century at least and striking for several reasons – not least its colossal chimneys that seem huge beyond any practical purpose. Maybe in those days the locals used chimneys as symbols of status and wealth, the way rich inhabitants of Italian renaissance towns competed with each other to build the tallest towers, often to absurd heights. It has a ramp leading to a large pair of doors on the first floor, presumably so that animals too could share the accommodation in winter. Although the building is now owned by the National Trust it isn't possible to visit it – at least not beyond the small shop from which the adjoining campsite is administered. This site stretches out spaciously along the lakeside, and is a picturesque place to camp, with the facilities of the town close at hand.

Coniston Hall: built when chimneys were a serious matter

The Old Man of Coniston

The big draw for the crowds is of course The Old Man of Coniston, the somewhat battered but noble mountain that sits behind the town. It is one of the easiest mountains in the Lakes to climb, for the main pathway up is broad and nowhere difficult, albeit very stony. And people do come, in huge numbers. Wainwright was characteristically grumpy about this: 'the day trippers, the courting couples, troops of earnest boy scouts, babies and grandmothers, the lot.' He drew a comic picture of them on the top, all trying to see Blackpool Tower, while the solitary walker to the side ('bless him') admires the hills. We can guess who that was.

The route from the town is signposted along the Walna Scar Road, but there is a more pleasant way along Church Beck (turn right at the Sun Hotel) that takes you past the old miners' bridge and a pretty waterfall. The path swerves to the left, away from the beck, and from then on it's pretty straightforward. The only cause for doubt might be at one place where the path divides and intuition seems to argue strongly for the right-hand path. Intuition is wrong, because this way leads round into the old quarry workings, and is not a way up. Take the left turn; almost immediately you will see the old quarry road joining from further to the left (the route via the Walna Scar Road comes in at this point) and after a sharp zig-zag the climb continues.

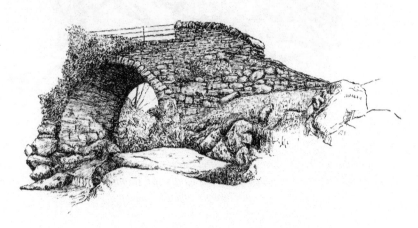

The Miners' Bridge

Anyone with their eyes open will by now have seen evidence of the widespread industrialisation of The Old Man, for the walk passes by and over heaps of waste from the slate quarrying that has taken place here for maybe eight hundred years, and which still continues a little way off in the valley below. Soon, the ground under your feet seems to consist of nothing but quarry spoil, while the walls on either side of the path are all built with quarry spoil. All around are stacks of debris, and huge steel cables – once used for hauling slate down the fellside – now lie discarded and rusting, so much junk. Out on a levelled platform, collapsed buildings are a roofless home to the rusting remains of the machinery once used by the quarrymen in their daily grind of winning the slate from the earth, cutting it and transporting it back to the village. Further on there are the rusting skeletons of toppled gantries, and cavernous holes where the slate was blasted out. It could hardly be called beautiful, but on a calm misty day there is a melancholic feel to the place, engendered by the evidence of so much human activity, now all gone, and the toll it took on the Old Man himself.

Collapsed gantry. Those twisting steel cables are a good two inches thick. The local Youth Hostel has a photograph of this gantry still standing, but age and the weather have brought about its downfall.

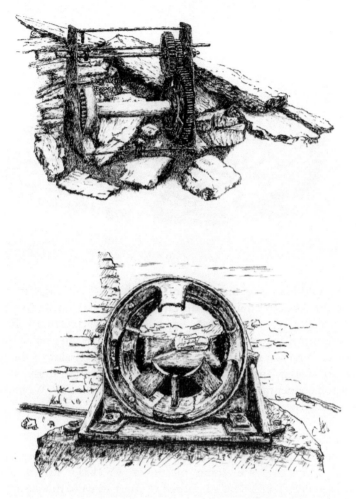

Abandoned machinery on the Old Man of Coniston

Once past the quarries it's not far to Low Water tarn, where you'll have earned a rest, and from there it's a fairly short but steep ascent up the last two hundred metres or so to the top. Here there is another surprise, for instead of the traditional cairn there's a great stone platform, with a sort of gateway into it, and a cairn standing on top. This took someone much time and effort to build – not something the average walker is likely to do now as he or she dashes about bagging peaks. From some angles it looks a little like a Mexican temple, but assuming the Aztecs weren't its architects, maybe the quarrymen had time on their hands one day and decided to build a grand monument for the mountain that gave them their livelihoods.

The summit cairn on the Old Man of Coniston

The Old Man is at the southern end of a first-rate ridge route that heads almost dead straight northwards, passing above Low Water and Levers Water up to Swirl How, where after a sharp left turn the ridge bends north again over Great Carrs and Little Carrs (and on all the way down to Wrynose Pass if you really want). It's level almost the whole way, so is easy and rewarding, with views over the crags into the Coniston copper mines valley and later, after Swirl How, to Wrynose and Little Langdale.

In Broad Slack, the gap between Great Carrs and Swirl How, there is something special. If you look closely at the craggy slopes below you might just see some pieces of wreckage strewn about inaccessibly. To the left, a hundred yards or so west, there is a large cairn, and if you approach it you will find that it's not a cairn at all, but a memorial to the crew of a wartime Halifax bomber that crashed here in 1944. The story is that the pilot got lost in mist and, flying too low, clipped the top of the fell and crashed. All eight crew, seven Canadians and one Scot – all but two of them aged 21 or under – were killed. The rescuers found the plane, and to prevent it being reported repeatedly by other pilots broke it up and pushed the pieces down Broad Slack. However, some parts from the undercarriage were kept and are now part of the memorial. If you look around there are chunks of metal, with signs of melting, embedded in the ground, rammed there by the force of the crash. On days with the mist swirling around and no sounds except the wind and an occasional croak from a raven, it's a sombre place.

The museum in Coniston tells the story more fully, and has one of the aircraft's engines on display.

The memorial on Great Carrs

If you turn back from Great Carrs meaning to return to Coniston, then the most direct route is probably off Swirl How down The Prison Band, which is not as daunting as it sounds. If you still feel energetic, then Wetherlam is right in front, and is fairly easily reached with surprisingly little ascent. However, on my last visit, frustrated by endless rain and low mist, I took the lower route past Levers Water into the Coppermines valley.

Levers Water is almost perfectly rectangular, and is another partly artificial tarn, having been dammed in the 19th century to provide water for the mines. The dam is still operational, its outflow tumbling over a weir and down Levers Water Beck into an area which is, well, a bit of a mess, because it's the centre of the old, defunct, copper mining industry and the modern operational slate mining.

Copper was mined here in earnest from the 16th century, although the industry seems to go back as far as the Romans. The Elizabethan miners were Germans, invited here because of their expertise and the growing demand in England for metals like copper and lead. They settled first at Keswick, but there was much resentment from the locals, and the Germans were obliged to live on an island in Derwent Water. But they were successful, working all over the Lake District, and their legacy still echoes in local surnames such as Mullen. From those beginnings the industry grew to an extraordinary scale. It's thought that at its peak in the mid-19th century as many as 600 people were employed at Coniston. These mines expanded until the deepest shafts went down 1,700 feet (520 metres), where the miners would have been working 600 feet (180 metres) below sea level. For most of the mines' existence there was no serious mechanisation, so to reach that depth the miners had to climb down ladders, working their way through a complicated network of shafts and passages several miles in length beneath the mountains. All the extraction was done using gunpowder and hand drills, with only candles for light; desperately hard work in this volcanic rock. Yet by 1850 so much ore was being extracted that a railway line was built to Coniston village to transport it away.

Cheap imports and increasingly difficult conditions as the seams became exhausted meant that even in the late 19th century the mines were going into decline, and most were shut early in the 20th century. The last one closed in the 1940s. Although some maps of the tunnels exist, many of the workings were forgotten, and are now being rediscovered by cavers and enthusiasts, who have found vast chasms, gaudily painted with brightly coloured mineral deposits, and deep, treacherous rifts opening out over drops of hundreds of feet. These mines are in a dangerous state, unsafe to enter without proper gear and guidance, but some, such as Levers Water mine, can be visited by appointment, with a guide.

Out on the surface, thousands of walkers pass by quite unaware of what is beneath their feet, but certainly aware of the piles of spoil around them, and the roughed-up state of the terrain.

Just below Levers Water you soon reach the site of Bonsor Mill, where more old machinery is on display: ore wagons set up on rails, crushing machines, weighing machines ... and an awful lot of miscellaneous rusting junk, recognisable only to the expert. The rather grand looking slate buildings once housed machinery, but have been converted to holiday homes, while a little further down is a more humble looking building, once accommodation for miners and now a Youth Hostel.

An old copper ore truck at Bonsor Mill

The whole area is dotted with entrances to abandoned mine workings — some carefully constructed, if somewhat ruinous now, and others little more than narrow gashes in the rock.

The entrance to an abandoned copper mine

The road down from Bonsor Mill and the Youth Hostel is easy and obvious, for it is kept in good enough condition for vehicles to use for access to the holiday cottages and the still operational slate mine up above the Mill. It soon reaches the Miners' Bridge, and from there Coniston is only a few minutes' walk away.

The Walna Scar Road

Isn't that a grand name? The Walna Scar Road. It sounds slightly foreboding: what is the scar? What, for that matter, does Walna mean? Is it a place, and what will happen when you get there?

In fact the Walna Scar Road is a rough track that crosses from Coniston to Dunnerdale, passing on the way over a rather dull rise called: Walna Scar. I first encountered it at the age of 17 with friends, on a hot summer's day, with Coniston Old Man before us and the lake behind. As we progressed the coast came into view, with the towers of Sellafield shadowed against the blue sea. We toiled over the low fells – the road never reaches a great height – until eventually we dropped down into the Duddon Valley, and went swimming in the river to cool off, gasping at its icy cold.

The road begins a little outside Coniston village, where you take the lane signposted to Coniston Old Man. You soon find yourself puffing up a steep incline that could be the hardest climb you'll face all day, even though it's asphalt. Eventually it levels off, crossing grassland until it reaches a wall and a car park – the furthest point that 'normal' cars can reach – before the Walna Scar Road proper begins.

The surface is good for walking on: rough in places but rarely at a steep gradient, and with a couple of well-built bridges. In the early 2000s it had become badly eroded, with large boulders blocking the way to most vehicles, but not walkers, and it was a favourite adventure ground for off-road bikers, who would churn up and down, trying not to break their necks. Even four-wheel drive vehicles would venture up there. More recently, and, to some, controversially, the road has been re-classified as a 'restricted byway', which means that the motor bikes and 4x4s are banned and it's left to walkers, horse riders and cyclists. But the controversy hasn't ended. The parks authority has carried out work to repair the damaged surface – made worse in the floods of 2009 – and now some cyclists are upset because they liked the challenge of the rough ride and don't want the (relatively) smooth surface they are now presented with. They're a rum lot; to my eyes there are still plenty of opportunities to come skidding off in a shower of sharp stones and rocks, leaving lumps of flesh and skin and broken machinery scattered behind you.

The Walna Scar Road

Apart from the cyclists, many walkers use the road as a way to reach either The Old Man or Dow Crag. There are several paths leading off to the Old Man; the old quarry road is the first, following the wall by the car park, leading to the main path up the Old Man via the old slate quarries. About a mile further on there's another, leading to a pleasant walk alongside Goats Water under the shadow of Dow Crag, followed by a steep ascent up the valley head to Goats Hawse, from where, after catching your breath, the route to the summit is obvious and easy.

Dow Crag

Later still, after skirting Brown Pike to the extent that you might think you've missed the path, there is a sharp turn to the right, just past a tiny stone shelter, that leads you up the back of Brown Pike and onto the long and thrilling ridge that runs directly north along Buck Pike and Dow Crag, with Blind Tarn and Goats Water far below. Dow Crag, with its deep gullies and sheer crags, is a favourite for rock climbers, but mere walkers will find even the track along its summit demanding from time to time, for it is very rocky. Beyond the Crag the ridge curves to the east, dropping a little to Goats Hawse and a crossing of paths. You can drop down to Goats Water from here, if weather or tired legs demand it, but a more satisfying day will be had if you continue on the long curving path that leads to the summit of the Old Man himself.

Stone shelter on the Walna Scar Road, next to the turn-off for Dow Crag

Brantwood

Coniston is famous for Donald Campbell and his fatal attempt to set a new water speed record in 1966. The museum in Coniston tells his story, ghoulishly playing a film of the moments when his jet-powered boat Bluebird crashed, in a continuous loop on a large TV screen. However, much more interesting and significant, to my mind at any rate, is the pinkish house you can see from Coniston jetty over on the wooded hillside on the opposite side of the lake, somewhat to the right. This is Brantwood, once the home of John Ruskin, one of the strangest, quirkiest and most brilliant intellectuals of the 19th century. Born in London in 1819, he rose to prominence as a young art critic, defending his hero JMW Turner at a time when the art world considered that the old boy had really lost his way.

If Ruskin had only been an art critic he might be forgotten now, but he was much more. He wrote about architecture, especially the Gothic style, and even now is remembered in Venice – a city he studied, drew and catalogued, stone by stone. He was a geologist, a highly accomplished draughtsman and watercolour painter, a professor of art who took his students out with picks and shovels to build a road, a lover of mountains, an energetic social campaigner, an evangelical protestant who lost his faith as he came to understand what geology was telling him about the real age of the earth, and perhaps most significant of all, a trenchant critic of the ugly side of 19th-century capitalism, writing savage attacks on greed and industrial exploitation of both people and nature.

He knew the Lake District well, having been brought there by his parents since he was a child; there is a memorial to him at Friars Crag, on Derwent Water, a place he wrote about many years later as an old man, describing his first visit there at the age of five. In 1871 he bought Brantwood without even seeing it, and set about improving and extending the house and its grounds. You can visit the house today, taking a ferry over Coniston Water from the village. It is as brilliant and strange as the man himself. He built a little glass tower with room for one person, in which he could stand and contemplate the mountains over the water and watch the clouds rolling in – clouds which, he was convinced, were blackened and poisoned by the smoke belching out of the chimneys of Manchester.

Over the years the trust that runs the house has gathered a collection of the paintings and writings that Ruskin himself kept there, and which had been sold and dispersed after his death; it is now a little treasure trove of Ruskin memorabilia.

Ruskin lived at Brantwood for nearly 30 years, the last ten virtually as a recluse, plagued by mental illness, and he died there in 1900. His grave is in the churchyard in Coniston village. Gandhi, Tolstoy, Proust and the founders of the Labour Party all admired him and were influenced by his ideas, but twenty years after his death he was almost forgotten – or ridiculed along with much else about the Victorian period. Now, with the separation of a century, he repays spending time with. I first discovered him one rain-soaked day when I visited Brantwood to escape the weather. That was over twenty years ago, and it was a lucky day.

The Coniston Museum also has an excellent display about Ruskin.

Ruskin's home, Brantwood

11 TWO PASSES AND THE DUDDON VALLEY

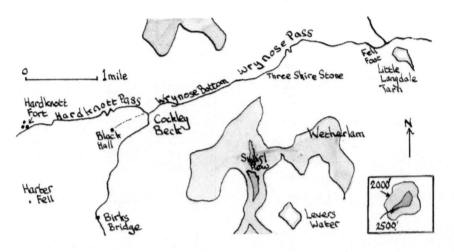

Wrynose and Hardknott

There was once a time when I was youthfully confident about taking on the toughest of the routes over the fells but genuinely nervous about driving over Wrynose and Hardknott passes. Now the situation is reversed: I've not so much suffered a loss of confidence about the fells than gained a greater sense of caution about them, but I now positively enjoy driving over those passes, even in torrential rain.

Taken together, Wrynose and Hardknott link the central area around Ambleside to Eskdale on the west – a fact not unknown to the Romans, who marched their soldiers back and forth along this route between Hardknott and Galava forts. You only have to look at a map for a few moments to see how this is the only direct road between the central area and the west; if you're in a car and don't fancy driving over these passes then you'll face a long roundabout route via Ulpha Fell, or, even longer, right round the northern fringes of the Lakes and down the coast road.

Travelling from the east, Wrynose comes first. There's a growing sense of anticipation as you approach: first you pass Fell Foot Farm, its whitewashed buildings jutting out into the road, forcing vehicles to pass at a crawl (and their passage presumably a constant source of disturbance to the occupants who might otherwise have thought they were out in remote wilderness); the landscape gets progressively bleaker; there are the road signs that leave nothing in doubt, with exclamation marks, warnings of severe bends, 30%

gradients and bans on all vehicles in winter conditions.

After the warning signs, the climb up the pass begins. To call it a road is to raise unrealistic expectations; it's a single-track way with a crumbling and potholed surface that winds and bends so much that at times it's lost to sight through the windscreen. There is some respite at the top, where the way is more or less level for half a mile or so, with small stopping places that provide handy jumping-off points for a quick ascent of Pike o' Blisco or over to Wetherlam. Then there's a steep winding descent to Wrynose Bottom, the long valley that runs for about a mile to Cockley Beck.

Wrynose Bottom often seems a forsaken place, even in summer when the sun and blue skies can transform the dullest scenery to splendour. Not so in Wrynose Bottom, which refuses to give up its cheerless air of desolation. Things brighten up a little at Cockley Beck, where a bridge crosses the bubbling River Duddon and there's a small farmhouse, whitewashed and with stone-framed rectangular windows.

For the driver, everything up to this point has been a preparation, the hors d'oeuvres before the main course: Hardknott. This is by far the more difficult of the two passes, laying its cards out immediately with a sharp right-hand bend onto a steep, banked, potholed ascent terminated by a hard left-hand bend to a bridge, its surface a mess of crumbling potholes that betray your tyres' grip just when you need it[17]. And it continues like this, twisting and turning, the banked curves often of an astounding steepness that make you wonder how the tarmac remains clinging to the earth's surface. In many places it doesn't, having become rippled under the drag of tyres, seriously reducing surface grip so if you try to accelerate through the result may be nothing more than noisy wheel spin and the smell of burning rubber.

Hardknott's road surface isn't always top grade

After much twisting and turning, with bends to the left switching into bends to the right so rapidly there's barely time to turn the steering wheel, the climb ends so abruptly that for a moment your front wheels are heading downwards while your rears are still on the way up.

Now the challenge is reversed, the gradients and bends just as severe but

---

[17] To be fair to the roads authority, this was the condition of the road in 2013; in 2014 it was tidily patched and resurfaced, with the holes all filled in.

with gravity propelling you down. There are two especially tricky hairpin bends that may challenge nerves, where you lose sight of the road in front while knowing that it just veered off to the left or right. They are even tougher on the way up.

Over the years I've learnt a few tricks about how to approach these passes. A long time ago, while contemplating them nervously, a friend and better driver than me said: just put it in first gear and keep going. That's not bad advice for the ascent, so long as you time dropping down to first gear correctly. (Leave it too late and you might find yourself close to stalling and at risk of losing precious momentum as you make a hasty gear change.) What you must avoid is stopping on the way up; the tense silence from your sweating passengers as you try to get moving again can be quite discomforting. Certainly a little practice helps; knowing those bends and how best to tackle them converts a nervy experience to one of pleasure. Modern cars are easier to drive than those of two or three decades ago and maybe first-timers today will wonder what all the fuss is about, but even with all that modern mechanical thrust to rely on there is still the matter of what to do when you meet someone coming the other way. The track is single lane with passing points just about wide enough to accommodate two vehicles side by side in a little motorised shuffle. On the way up you really need to rely on the common sense of drivers coming down, hoping they will see you and wait for you to pass. Which, by and large, they do. And on the way down, well, just keep a lookout well ahead.

If you have passengers they may now be distracting you by exclaiming at the view of Eskdale that has opened up – assuming they aren't sitting with their eyes covered – a view you will be too preoccupied to enjoy. But there it is, not at all like Wrynose Bottom, but a classically composed water-colourist's landscape with forests and rocky promontories and a river and clouds and the gleaming sea far in the distance.

Hardknott eventually gives way and before long you cross a cattle grid and a gate through a wall, and the landscape changes completely as you enter the broad and gentle Eskdale Valley. But what may have been missed on the way down is the Roman fort perched up on the fells on the right-hand side of the road. You can't see it from the road, but it is surprisingly large, a walled rectangle containing the remains of accommodation, a granary and administrative buildings, with a bathhouse a little way off down the slope, and even the remains of a parade ground. The walls are up to six feet high, and while first thoughts are that they must surely have been rebuilt – ancient buildings were often ransacked for building materials in the past – this is not so. There is a visible line of stone embedded high up in the walls marking the height of the Roman remains. Everything above has been added in modern times, but the old walls have survived remarkably well to a significant height. It's thought that the fort was built in the second century and stationed 500 men of the fourth Cohort of Dalmatians, exiles from the sunny Adriatic coast sent to endure the winters and rains of northern Britain.

The gateway to the Roman fort, with Hardknott Pass in the background

Famously, the Romans did not build bendy roads, and sure enough, back over on the Cockley Beck side the Ordnance Survey map shows a Roman Road running dead straight south-west along the river plain to a farmhouse named Black Hall. The ancient road is now the route to the farm, and you can walk along it. Now, almost invariably in the Lake District footpaths go right through farm yards, winding between the house and barns and stores – something that can feel a bit intrusive. But things are different at Black Hall, for Black Hall specialises in mad dogs. As you approach, long before reaching the buildings, they start barking. By the time you reach the outskirts they are worked up into a crazy frenzy, filled with fury at your impertinence. The path does not go through this farmyard but skirts around the buildings in a wire mesh tunnel that must only have been put there to protect walkers from the canines. The creatures hurl themselves at the wire, but while they may be mad they are also in bad shape: old, scruffy and with unseeing misty blue eyes. Once, after I passed the farm, one of them broke out and came running after me barking angrily. I turned and readied myself to floor it with a boot if need be, but, like all bullies, it was a coward, and a pointed arm and a stern 'home!' was all it took to see it off.

How things change. Many years ago Black Hall was a youth hostel, one of the Simple Grade hostels – a concept that was swept away long ago as the YHA tried to attract a new generation by offering carpets, bars and car parks. My friends and I stayed here in the long hot summer of my 18th year, and my main recollection now is not of aggressive dogs but of the washing facilities: a pile of plastic washing-up bowls and a cold tap out in the yard.

The OS map loses the Roman road shortly after the farm, but it's fairly clear where it went. There is a path that climbs up the hillside and soon joins a broad track that meets the Hardknott road at the summit. This must surely be the route the Romans used, and very sensible of them it was too, for it's easy to see that the gradient by this route is much less than via Hardknott – the difference between a practical route built by engineers to serve soldiers marching in armour, and the Chestertonian 'crooked road an English drunkard made' that we have now.

Galava fort, by the way, can still be seen on the edge of Ambleside. It is located in a very pretty place close to the lake shore where the rivers Brathay and Rothay meet before flowing into Windermere, with Loughrigg Fell as a backdrop. The nearby A5075 is a modern addition.

The Duddon Valley

Cockley Beck is a three-way junction connecting Wrynose Bottom to the east, Hardknott to the west, and the Duddon Valley to the south. Harter Fell, in the western corner, offers some interesting rocky landscape to explore on its summit, but its eastern flanks overlooking the River Duddon are in the tender care of the Forestry Commission and are not so pleasant to walk in, consisting mostly of rows of identical fir trees and muddy ditches made by heavy machinery. Recently, large areas have been felled, leaving an empty and desolate landscape, but it's hoped that this is a temporary state of affairs, for the intention is to replant the whole area with oak and birch, interspersed with bogs and open ground. In other words, to return it to something like it was before the great plantations were introduced in the 1930s.

The desolation left behind after the trees have been felled looks a little like an old World War One battlefield. However, if all goes to plan, this will be temporary.

Down by the river, there are attractive walks and interesting things to be found, notably Birks Bridge, which arches between the rocky sides of a narrow gorge where the Duddon's waters are forced into fast-flowing turbulence. Construction must have been difficult, not to say dangerous. Not so far away the river is wider and flows more slowly, while its banks are lower. Such places look like easier options, but the builders knew that those rock banks provided the firm foundations needed to support the bridge's arch and the weight of its stone, and that built here it would last far longer, and be safer against winter floods, than if they had chosen lower ground.

Birks Bridge: a perfect piece of engineering in stone

Wordsworth wrote much about the Duddon Valley, or, as he preferred to call it, Dunnerdale, including this advice:

All hail, ye mountains! hail, thou morning light!
Better to breathe at large on this aëry height
Than toil in needless sleep from dream to dream

Exactly so: come on, get up out of bed and out to the fells!

12 ENDNOTES

Paths

Back in the 1980s it was becoming clear that many of the paths on the fells were being destroyed. Pounded by thousands of boots, the turf and soil was loosened and then washed away by the rain, exposing rough rubble. As walkers used the edges of the damaged paths to avoid the roughness and sprained ankles, they spread the erosion and the paths widened into ugly scars across the fellsides many yards wide, difficult to walk on, sometimes dangerous. I remember struggling up a badly damaged path on Black Sail Pass at Wasdale Head with friends and being rebuked by a gloomy walker coming the opposite way. 'You're not on the path,' he muttered as we passed, but how he could tell among the mess of sliding stones and mud, none of us knew.

We would worry about this afterwards in the pub, and wonder what could be done. 'Management,' said one of our number, just about to embark on a management career. That sounded promising; what did he have in mind? Regrettably, details were hazy.

Fortunately, other people with a more practical turn of mind were also working on the problem. Although it took several years while they debated the options and looked at experience elsewhere, the National Park Authority, the National Trust and English Nature got together and embarked on a long-term programme of path building. This was a huge undertaking; they began by drawing up a list of 145 paths that needed repair, and set to work, aiming to fix fourteen every year for ten years. The paths were rebuilt, yard by yard, using stone and muscle, often by volunteer labour. It is very hard physical work, carried out in difficult conditions; the 'Fix the Fells' website says the qualities needed for the job are 'stamina, endurance, strength … and an artistic eye' – the latter because after all, the new paths aren't just functional, they're intended to add to the beauty of the area[18].

One can only admire the dedication of the people who did this, and continue to do it, and thank them for such a successful endeavour. For the effects are quite dramatic. The new paths are sturdy, with stones set into the ground so that they're firm underfoot and never move. The soil and vegetation has been stabilised, and the old scars are disappearing as the grass

---

[18] I cannot decide if that includes the path on Sail.

198

and ferns and moss return. The paths are good to walk on[19], and of course they make it much less likely that you'll get lost. And because they channel walkers along them, they reduce damage to other paths that have not been reconstructed. The last time I climbed the old Rossett Gill path in Langdale, some years ago, it was the usual sad picture of destruction, with parts of the path almost impassable because of the damage. The route entailed a steep climb up the waterway, but people had been forced to climb further and further up the sides of the gully to gain a safe foothold, and in so doing had spread the damage ever wider. Now, there's a stone path that zig-zags its way up the old pony route to the left of the Gill, and the damaged path is almost unused. True, you do not see the Gill until the stone route brings you to a viewpoint right above it, and then you see the old path – or rather do not see it, because it has virtually disappeared under new vegetation. It is an example of nature's power to self-mend, perhaps with a little help from the Park Authority.

In the early days you would occasionally hear people complain about these paths: they diminish the experience, it's not the same, etc. Well, it is true that it's not the same, and if anyone needs a reminder of what it used to be like there are still some paths in a shocking state of disrepair, usually very high up or in places that are nigh impossible to fix (Lord's Rake, anyone?). The days of wandering freely over the fells are largely gone because of the numbers of people who now walk there, but these paths mean that visitors can come and walk guilt-free, to enjoy one of the most beautiful places in England, or, indeed, anywhere.

---

[19] That is true nearly everywhere, but as I've occasionally grumbled in this book, there are exceptions. Some are built far too steeply, without zig-zags, while too many have their surfaces set at the wrong angle. The path that snakes around the western flank of Pike o' Blisco, leading down from Red Tarn to Oxendale, has the flat surfaces of its stones all sloping downwards. This makes it easy and comfortable to walk up, but quite something else going down. The sloping surface is difficult enough in dry conditions, but slippery and genuinely dangerous in the wet – especially when lubricated with sloppy dollops of sheep muck. I make this claim based on experience and a bruised backside.

Part of the path up Stickle Ghyll in Langdale. It may look like a rock garden path, but those stones are massive, and they aren't going to budge for a very long time.

Rain

You have to face up to it: if you come to the Lakes you are likely to get wet. The clouds roll in off the Irish Sea to collide with the mountains and the result is rain – a lot of it. It rains here on roughly 220 days per year, or two out of three days. Seathwaite, in Borrowdale, has the dubious distinction of being the wettest inhabited place in England, with 3400mm per year, or about 135 inches. That is over eleven feet, almost the combined height of two men: it's worth thinking about that for a moment.

But there is worse. There is a rain gauge at Sprinkling Tarn that recorded 6,527mm of rain in 1954, a miserable year for sheep and walkers. Nearby, Styhead Tarn has the highest average annual rainfall, at 4,391mm.

So the sound of rain drumming on your hood is just one of the things you have to get used to, and all you can do is buy good-quality waterproofs and remember that it's rarely as bad as you imagine once you're outside. It can even be quite pleasant for an hour or two, until the streaming water starts to find ways into your clothing and boots. Light or even moderately heavy rain, especially on the lower levels, can be a real pleasure as it falls, sparkling on the ferns and grass, dripping from the trees and releasing a fresh, heady odour of earth, rocks and life: petrichor is the word for it.

In his *Guide to the Lakes*, Wordsworth wrote that 'the rain here comes down heartily', but went on to describe how, so often, 'it is succeeded by clear, bright weather, when every brook is vocal, and every torrent sonorous'. Regular walkers will recognise this description.

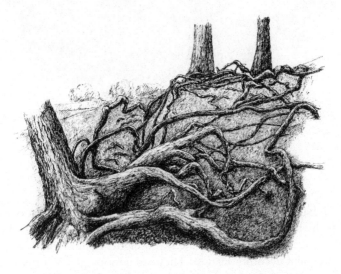

Tree-roots on the shores of Derwent Water, exposed by the lapping waters of the lake

The obvious truth is that rain is essential to the form and character of the Lake District. Running water and its opposite, ice, have shaped this landscape for millennia and continue to do so. Huge glaciers carved out the valleys thousands of years ago, and ice continues to work away quietly, splitting rocks or nudging boulders downhill as the ground freezes and thaws. The rivers, streams and becks carry away tiny particles of rock and soil, constantly nibbling away at the land, reforming it and moving water courses – often in a perpetual battle with man, valiantly trying to keep things in place. And it generates a rich flora that is quite distinctive of the Lakes, with thick green mosses and ferns spread over rocks and walls alike. When leaving, after a few days spent walking, one of the surest signs that the holiday is over is the sudden absence of those thick mosses and ferns from the landscape.

A mossy wall. The abundantly rich mosses and ferns are characteristic of the Lakes, and a direct result of its wet climate.

Accommodation

Although I have stayed in B&Bs, and I still think that in good weather camping is the best way to experience the Lakes if you want to feel the earth and see the true starry darkness of the sky at night, Youth Hostels have been my most frequent accommodation. They are curious places, often in once-grand country houses set in spectacular locations such that if they were hotels they would cost a small fortune to stay in. As it is, they are usually a bit shabby and pervaded by an immediately recognisable Youth Hostel smell: the odour of maturing sweat and socks, absorbed and re-emitted by the carpets that were installed thirty years ago to try to attract a new generation. So yes, they can be a little basic, but for me their great appeal is that you will always be among other walkers with tales to tell, and that you usually have the complete run of a building – often large and idiosyncratic, maybe even with its own grounds. That beats staying in an overheated B&B with fluffy carpets in the bathroom.

It's true that the epithet 'Youth' is not wholly accurate these days, if it ever was. There are periods, especially during school term times, when some hostels seem like outposts of The University of The Third Age, and even during school holidays the number of young people – by which I mean teenagers and young people travelling independently – seems small[20] . There is no problem with older people using the hostels of course; no doubt their business is welcome, and they know the value of experiencing the mountains and countryside directly with boots and cagoule. No, it's just that the relative absence of younger people seems a little sad, especially in an organisation that was originally set up to appeal to them. Maybe the concept is dated now, and the idea of sharing a bedroom and even a bunk with people you've never met before, of which at least one will snore all night, just doesn't cut it anymore.

This has had some consequences. While there has always been a slow turnover in hostels, with new buildings coming into use and others dropping out, in 2011 three Lake District hostels were put up for sale in the same year. Derwentwater was one; a fabulous slate-built house standing in its own grounds on the eastern shore of the lake. This is the house built by Joseph Pocklington, the man who made a business out of his tall stories about the Bowder Stone a couple of miles away in Borrowdale. Then there was Thorney How in Grasmere, and Elterwater. They were all closed because the accountants could not see how to make them profitable, but in all three cases the businesses were taken over by groups of people, some of them ex-YHA staff, determined to run them as independent hostels. So far they seem to be successful, with money invested in the buildings, and new ideas about how to raise standards and attract visitors. One wishes them well.

---

[20] Not helped by the rule, no doubt imposed for legal reasons, that you must be aged 18 or more to stay at a hostel on your own. However, 16 year-olds can stay, so long as they are in a group.

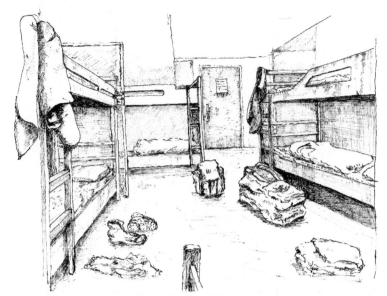

Inside the hostel dormitory

Holding your nerve

Back in the days when I went walking the fells with university friends there was one of our group who was, let's say, a little less agile than the rest of us. We would make fun of his clumsy attempts to get over stepping stones that nearly always ended with him standing with one foot in the water. We could all see where he was going wrong: it was his hesitation. He would pause with one foot on a rock, delaying just for a moment while working out what to do next, but in that fraction of a second his balance would be lost and the other foot would have to come down somewhere. What he needed was the momentum to keep going without dithering, never keeping a foot on one stone long enough for it to matter if it wobbled, propelled from one to the next in an elegant continuum of motion.

His intellect knew this, but knowing it wasn't enough to make it happen.

Now, three decades later, I find that my confidence in my own feet and legs is less than it was and I've caught myself doing exactly what my old friend did, being over-cautious and hesitating. This had to stop. So, if you find yourself in this situation, here's what to do. By all means take a few moments – but no more than that – to work out what your next moves will be before committing to whatever difficult manoeuvre you face: the sequence of stepping stones, the hand-holds, whatever it is. Then say out loud to yourself, 'One, Two, Three, Go!' and really go. Do not, under any circumstances, hesitate, just go. It's guaranteed to work, every time.

ABOUT THE AUTHOR

John Swanson hails from the North East of England, but spent a happy
early childhood in Cumbria. He is married and lives in South West London.
His wife and three sons have tolerated his Lake District obsession with
cheerful patience for many years.